D1161459

101
RIDING
EXERCISES

THE ESSENTIAL GUIDE TO IMPROVING EVERY ASPECT OF YOUR RIDING

KAREN BUSH

and

JULIAN MARCZAK

FABRS

D&C
David and Charles

I dedicate this book to my four outstanding teachers: the late Charles Harris, Daniel Pevsner, the late Nuño Oliveira and Philippe Davenport, who educated and inspired me in their individual, unique ways. For this I owe them immeasurable gratitude.

Julian Marczak FABRS

Acknowledgments

With thanks to Sarah Fisher for introducing me to TTouch, which has proved an invaluable teaching aid, and of course I am indebted to all my long suffering teachers over the years. Thanks are also due to Jackie Forster and Harvey, who gave their time and patience so generously to pose as artist's models for the exercises, to Jane Trollope at David & Charles, my Project Editor Anne Plume and Maggie Raynor who translated all the photos into drawings.

Karen Bush

The authors would like to thank the following for their input and comments while reading through the manuscript during preparation of this book: Suzanne Marczak FABRS; Shirley Renowden FABRS; Lt Col (Retd) Gordon Wesley FABRS, BHS(SMT), ABRS Prin Dip, NSBD.

A DAVID & CHARLES BOOK
Copyright © David & Charles Limited 2009

David & Charles is an F+W Media Inc. company
4700 East Galbraith Road
Cincinnati, OH 45236

First published in the UK and USA in 2009

Text copyright © Karen Bush and
Julian Marczak 2009

Illustrations by Maggie Raynor copyright ©
David & Charles Limited 2009

Photographs copyright © Horsepix 2009. With its roots in horse country and staffed by horse people, Horsepix is a leading provider of high quality equestrian photography.

Karen Bush and Julian Marczak have asserted their right to be identified as authors of this work in accordance with the Copyright, Designs and Patents Act, 1988.

Horse care and riding are not without risk, and while the author and publishers have made every attempt to offer accurate and reliable information to the best of their knowledge and belief, it is presented without any guarantee. The authors and publishers therefore disclaim any liability incurred in connection with using the information contained in this book.

A catalogue record for this book is available from the British Library.

ISBN-13: 978-0-7153-3147-7 hardback
ISBN-10: 0-7153-3147-7 hardback

Printed in Singapore by KHL
for David & Charles
Brunel House   Newton Abbot   Devon

Commissioning Editor: Jane Trollope
Desk Editor: Emily Rae
Assistant Editor: Joanna Richards
Project Editor: Anne Plume
Senior Designer: Jodie Lystor
Design Assistant: Victoria Marks
Production Controller: Beverley Richardson

Visit our website at www.davidandcharles.co.uk

David & Charles books are available from all good bookshops; alternatively you can contact our Orderline on 0870 9908222 or write to us at FREEPOST EX2 110, D&C Direct, Newton Abbot, TQ12 4ZZ (no stamp required UK only); US customers call 800-289-0963 and Canadian customers call 800-840-5220.

CONTENTS

FOREWORD

101 Riding Exercises is a must for every riding enthusiast. It is a fund of equestrian knowledge, of great use to both teachers and pupils of all standards and provides a mass of information to help every rider to reach their goal.

Laid out in easily understood jargon, each exercise is explained simply and concisely with tips on how to derive the maximum benefit from each one and how to avoid making mistakes. The clear and informative drawings add to the script with their clarity and simplicity. Every part of the rider's body is covered from head to toe, to ensure that all who read and use it gain the maximum from its pages. It is also full of fascinating quotes and tips from experts past and present.

The Troubleshooting section deals with common problems and how to put them right – invaluable to every equestrian who wants to excel at their chosen sport. The emphasis is on the correct position throughout the book – if you do not master this first, every part of your body is likely to be affected and become unbalanced. This is not only going to affect the effectiveness of the rider, but also the horse's way of going.

The book covers such basics as the clothing worn, the importance of safety at all times, balance and coordination, correct breathing, emotional issues, as well as dismounted exercises for everyday use.

Riding is a wonderfully healthy sport that can be undertaken by all age groups. It combines a special bond and companionship between horse and human, unique to the sport. It also provides a form of exercise that literally affects every muscle and nerve in the body as the rider learns to move in unison with their partner, the horse.

The authors, both experts in their field and very well known in the horse world, have managed to produce a concise and well laid out record of basic and essential knowledge, which combines a huge amount of information and guidance.

Julian Marczak and Karen Bush's book is a masterpiece of useful and absorbing information that fills a much-needed gap in essential reading for every rider and trainer of all standards. I have found it enormously stimulating and informative; as I am sure will all who read and learn from *101 Riding Exercises*.

Jane Holderness-Roddam

Jane Holderness-Roddam was born in Catherston, near Charmouth in Dorset. In 1968 she achieved sporting fame by winning Badminton on her horse 'Our Nobby'; this was followed by her selection for the Olympics in Mexico the same year. There she became the first British woman to compete in the Olympic three-day event, and won a Team Gold medal. She has since ridden, judged, instructed and competed in many countries around the world and made a major contribution to equestrian sport, to the promotion of related education and training, and to improving the welfare of horses and ponies.

Her horses also included 'Warrior', who carried her to victory at Burghley in 1976, the Team Gold at the European Championships at Burghley in 1977 and to victory again at Badminton in 1978. Following her retirement from 'event riding' in the mid 1990s, Jane remains involved as President of British Eventing, as well as the Fortune Centre of Riding Therapy. She is also currently Chairman of Riding for the Disabled Association (RDA) and the National Riding Festival.

INTRODUCTION

'Some people, who do not know that arena work is necessary in horsemanship, say "Do I have to do all these movements?"'

Gaspard de Saunier 1663–1748: French soldier, equestrian and author on classical horsemanship

Virtually the first thing you are taught as a beginner is the correct way in which to sit when mounted; ideally, trying to achieve as perfect a position as possible should then continue to be an ongoing goal throughout your riding career, since whatever your aspirations, correct posture is the foundation that underpins everything you do. It also determines to a large extent the level of your success and how much pleasure you derive from your horse.

Placing position high on the list of rider priorities is not a new idea – indeed, its importance has been emphasized by all the great riding masters from ancient times right through to the modern day – but it is an aspect that very often tends to be neglected, to the cost of horse as well as rider. The key benefits of a correction position include the following:
- safety – you are less likely to fall off
- good, clear communication with the horse
- it is more comfortable for the rider …
- … and more comfortable for the horse
- the rider is better able to 'read' the horse and to anticipate any problems
- it is more efficient and less tiring
- it reduces the likelihood of injury being incurred by either horse or rider.

A poor position, on the other hand, can be responsible for all sorts of problems, including the following:
- it can lead to many evasions
- it opens the way for undesirable and unnecessary battles
- it may cause feelings of insecurity and ineffectiveness, which can be confidence sapping, and increase any nervousness you may feel

- it can lead to confusing and conflicting aids and, even if your horse does understand what you want him to do, it can make it difficult for him to comply
- it is frequently responsible for creating 'problem' horses – if you run into any difficulties, rider position should always be checked sooner rather than later as a possible cause
- it will certainly limit your ability to progress, since until you have mastered your own posture it is hard to educate your horse in the correct use of his.

Anyone can learn to sit well; depending on individual body shape this may be more challenging for some than others, but it certainly isn't an insurmountable problem and personal conformation shouldn't be used as an excuse for failing to do the best you can. Using exercises such as those described in this book will help you – however, you should always

be aware that there are no shortcuts or magic wands, and improvement does require determination and self-discipline, particularly when trying to overcome established bad habits.

Ultimately, however, it will all be worth the effort. As well as being able to realize your own potential and that of your horse, there is nothing to equal the exhilarating, uplifting and almost spiritual experience of truly working in harmony with each other, the horse an easy and willing extension of your own body and mind.

TIP

Working on position needn't be a boring chore, but can be incorporated into everyday activities as well as when riding and as a part of your warm-up.

THE BASICS

'The good rider must be able to lay claim to an education. Then he also feels the need to analyse his actions. He will try to deduce them from nature by scientific means, and form a system that can serve as a foundation for all his individual actions.'

Louis Seeger 1798–1865: German riding master and author on classical horsemanship

CONTENTS

A good position is not something that is immediately acquired – it takes time to achieve and longer to establish – but neither is it something elusive and obtainable only by the most dedicated and experienced riders. Everyone, from the most novice to the most advanced of riders, has the capacity to improve their position, and the rewards are both evident and worth working for, such as better responses from the horse, or simply feeling more comfortable. We owe it to our horses to be the very best we can.

Comfort for rider and horse

If you aren't comfortable, or if your movement is restricted by what you're wearing, your position and safety will suffer accordingly. Riding wear today is designed to be fashionable as well as to provide comfort, protection and freedom of movement, so there's really no excuse for not wearing appropriate clothing. Nevertheless, there are a few areas where it's still possible to slip up.

Rider clothing

- Avoid overlong boots, which can give your legs the flattering appearance of being longer and slimmer. Unless sufficiently cut away, they can also rub painfully at the back of your knees, encouraging you to ride with stirrups too long or with insufficiently flexed knee joints – what feels fine standing upright while trying them on in a shop can be very different when you are actually riding.
- When buying new riding clothes, don't try to squeeze yourself into too small a size, even if it is with the optimistic expectation of losing some weight.
- The right sort of underwear is important and not always given enough attention; ladies should avoid lacy knicker trims, thongs and underwired bras, while men may find either briefs or stretch boxers with sculptured front panels the most comfortable option.

Saddle fit

Saddle fit is an equally important consideration. Although the horse's requirements are quite rightly taken into account, the needs of the rider are equally important but sometimes overlooked. If the saddle isn't a good fit for the rider too, it can be a cause of poor position, which in turn can cause the horse discomfort. You should check:

- the length and breadth of the seat
- the position and shape of the knee and thigh rolls
- the placement of the stirrup bars.

All of these can have a direct and dramatic effect on rider position for better or worse. Therefore, when buying a new saddle, try riding in it in all gaits before you decide to purchase it, and if possible have your teacher on hand to help advise on this aspect.

The ideal position

You can improve your position in a number of ways. These might include using various physical exercises, increasing body awareness, lunge lessons, breathing techniques and through visualization, but before embarking on any of these you first need to have a clear idea in your own mind of exactly what it is you are aiming for.

❏ **Alignment** Seen from the side, it should be possible to draw an imaginary perpendicular line through the rider's ear, shoulder, hip and heel. It should also be possible to trace a straight line from the elbow, along the forearm and reins to the horse's mouth. Viewed from the front or rear, a perpendicular line dropped from the top of the head to the ground should bisect the body into two equal halves, with the rider's spine directly above that of the horse.
❏ **Seat** Sit squarely in the deepest, most central part of the saddle with the weight equally distributed across both seat bones, buttocks and thighs. The hip bones should be vertical and directly beneath the shoulders.
❏ **Head** The head should be level, looking straight ahead with the chin in line with the breastbone.

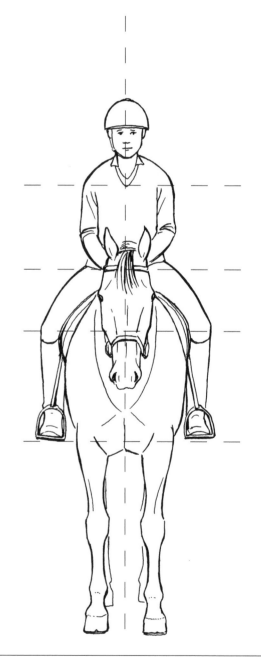

❏ **Torso** The torso should be vertical, in balance, be elegant and supple, without any slumping or hollowing of the lower back; firm without being stiff, flexible without being floppy.

❏ **Shoulders** Keep the shoulder blades flat, with the shoulders stretched open and level with each other.

❏ **Arms** Have the upper arms hanging lightly by your sides, with the elbows flexed and close to, but not clamped against, the body.

❏ **Hands** Hold the hands level with each other above the withers, the width of the bit apart, with the backs facing outwards and the thumbs uppermost.

❏ **Legs** From the thigh to mid-calf the legs should lie in a close, but not tight, contact with the horse's sides, with the thigh at an angle of approximately 45 degrees and lying as flat as possible against the saddle. Both knees should appear to be the same height when viewed from the front.

❏ **Feet** The feet should lie parallel to the horse's sides and level with each other, with the balls placed squarely on the tread of the stirrup irons. The heels should be the same height as, or slightly lower than, the toes.

Learning tools

It's one thing to be aware of what constitutes a correct position, but trying to achieve it is quite another – this may involve 'unlearning' bad habits, and the coordination, strength, balance and suppleness required is sometimes hard to master. Your body can also deceive you very convincingly that you are doing something in a certain way when in reality this isn't the case. A good example is that of a rider who habitually tends to tip forward, but when encouraged to sit in a more correct upright position, it's likely they'll feel as if they are leaning backwards. This illustrates not only how difficult it can sometimes be to detect a positional problem, but also to know exactly how far you need to go in order to correct it. However, there are various ways you can solve this.

❏ **Photography** Photographs can be most helpful in analysing faults and as a teaching aid. They allow you to relate visually to what you feel when asked to make a correction by your teacher.
   ❏ Digital cameras mean you can view pictures on screen straight after they have been taken.
   ❏ Camcorders are better still, as they don't rely on someone pressing the shutter at precisely the right moment, and you can watch a whole sequence rather than a series of stills. As with digital cameras, they can be replayed immediately for analysis or confirmation. Initially you may be a little self-conscious, but after a few sessions this will wear off.
   ❏ If recordings are kept, they can also serve as a form of riding diary, allowing you to see how you are progressing over a period of time, and to spot the appearance of any undesirable habits.
❏ **Mirrors** If available, mirrors can be useful in helping you to assess your posture, particularly your straightness as you ride directly towards one. They should be made of toughened glass, mounted securely at a minimum height of 1.8m (6ft), and tilted at a slight angle so they can be used from the opposite side of the school.

❏ **Help from the ground** This is one of the best options of all, especially if your helper is a good teacher. In between lessons, even a novice or entirely 'non-horsy' person can provide you with valuable information, as long as you first explain to them exactly what you'd like them to observe and comment on.
❏ **Equine simulator** In addition to, or as an alternative to, lunge lessons, and accompanied by tuition from a teacher, a simulator can be a great help in improving and establishing posture. The most recent models are fairly sophisticated, and in addition to producing relatively realistic gaits, can respond to rein and leg aids, offer computerized feedback, and provide the opportunity to practise as much as you want without risk of boring or tiring the horse. The main drawback is that although their use is increasing, there still aren't many around as yet; and it will still be necessary to learn how to transfer the skills learnt to the real thing, which can never be entirely satisfactorily imitated.

Further help

Adopting a correct posture in the saddle is easier if you already have a correct, balanced and coordinated posture on the ground, so it may be worth exploring complementary modalities that can help. Some can aid in developing patience and mental self-discipline, which are equally important requirements in riding. You may discover other modalities too, but the following are all widely accepted as being beneficial for riders, and also mesh well with the principles of sound riding practice.

- ❏ **Alexander Technique** Devised by actor Frederick Matthias Alexander, it has an obvious appeal for riders because the techniques focus on achieving an upright, poised and elegant posture, that is free of rigidity. It improves coordination, balance and breathing, increases self-awareness, releases tension, and teaches a more efficient and effortless way of moving.
- ❏ **Feldenkrais** Developed by Dr Moshe Feldenkrais, this method uses gentle, non-habitual movements to create increased postural awareness, helps overcome ingrained undesirable actions, and aids in achieving efficient, coordinated movement using minimal effort.
- ❏ **Pilates** Developed by Joseph Pilates, this has become popular with riders to improve fitness. The main principles are improving the support of proper posture and position of the spine with the deep muscles of the back and abdomen, and promoting efficient balance and movement of the arms and legs.
- ❏ **TTouch** Devised by Linda Tellington-Jones, and also known as TTEAM, this method views the body as a whole, recognizing that posture can influence attitude, emotions and behaviour, and vice versa. A system of groundwork, bodywork and riding exercises is used, which influences the nervous system, integrates body and mind, and improves coordination and balance.
- ❏ **Yoga** A useful form of exercise for riders that helps to relieve stress, placing emphasis on balance, body tone and mental and physical awareness. Tension, tightness and stiffness in the body are countered by gently flexing joints and lengthening soft tissues; breathing techniques also play an important part.

Tools to avoid

Two thousand years ago Xenophon, the first writer on equitation, wrote 'What a horse does under compulsion he does blindly …' – and the same principle applies to riders. The use of gadgets and positional aids that push and hold the rider into an approximation of a correct position is to be avoided at all costs:
- ❏ excessively deep and short-seated saddles
- ❏ prominent knee and thigh rolls
- ❏ angled stirrup irons.

The rider becomes mentally and physically reliant on them and doesn't learn how to maintain a correct posture without their aid; and can cause injuries if muscles and joints are excessively stressed. In addition, some do not allow for variation in individual build, can distort the posture, and can also fix the position, creating tension and stiffness. As well as gadgets, avoid dangerous practices – for example, that of tying stirrup irons to the girth to try and maintain lower leg stability.

Fitness

Being fit is as important for riders as for their horses – you don't need to turn yourself into a super-athlete, but taking stock of your level of fitness and doing something to increase it if necessary will be mutually beneficial for both you and your horse. Being fitter will enable you to keep going for longer, more safely and comfortably, with better control over your body and consequently over your horse; it'll be easier to maintain a correct position, and you'll be less likely to suffer from aches and pains afterwards. Your horse will also tire less quickly if he's not burdened by a fatigued rider, the risk of injury will be reduced, and through being more comfortable he will be more likely to be a willing partner.

GETTING A STITCH

Although there are a great many theories, no one is entirely sure what causes a 'stitch' – the sharp stabbing pain under the lower edge of the ribcage, which sometimes occurs during activities such as running or riding. It does, however, appear to be more likely to occur if you ride too soon after eating, so it's sensible to allow a sufficient gap following a meal. If you do get a stitch, stop what you are doing and breathe slowly, regularly and deeply, and you should find that the discomfort passes fairly quickly. If the stitch doesn't go away, or recurs during rest, seek medical attention.

Cardiovascular workouts

If you look after your horse yourself, doing yard work will help; however, it can increase one-sidedness, and isn't enough by itself anyway. You need to include cardiovascular workouts and exercises to improve strength, balance, flexibility and muscle tone. Ideally you should try to include some kind of a cardiovascular workout for 20–30 minutes at least three times a week; raising your pulse and respiratory rate increases heart and lung capacity, builds stamina, boosts energy and as an added bonus helps reduce body fat. If you find you don't have time, split it into shorter chunks – three 10-minute sessions instead of one 30-minute one, for example. You can also incorporate exercise into your everyday routine – walking briskly or cycling to work or the shops perhaps, and taking the stairs instead of the lift.

Strength and suppleness

A certain amount of correctly developed strength is also necessary, but weight training shouldn't be overdone – aim to tone rather than build muscle, which can actually create problems. Advice from an expert is helpful; you can ask for suggestions as to suitable exercises to build strength in the lower back and abdominal muscles, to supple the thighs and calves, and increase flexibility in the joints. The help of a trainer will also ensure that you learn how to use any gym equipment safely.

Increasing suppleness can be achieved through the use of stretching exercises – Chapter 17 contains a few suggestions.

❑ Exercises performed incorrectly are worse than not doing them at all – learn how to do them properly.

❑ Dress suitably for whatever you're doing – for activities such as jogging, skipping or aerobics, make sure that you wear properly designed trainers that offer support to your feet and absorb shock.

❑ If you have any health issues, consult your doctor before starting any exercise programme.

❑ Build your fitness slowly and sensibly – pushing your body too hard and too quickly invites injury.

❑ Warm up properly before doing any exercise so your body is properly prepared and less likely to be injured.

❑ Warm down after exercise too; this helps to remove lactic acid from the muscles and allows the heart rate to return to normal gradually, thereby reducing the stress on it.

❑ **Trampolining** Amongst other benefits, trampolining improves cardiovascular fitness and increases coordination, flexibility, agility and reaction times. NASA astronauts even use it to increase their body control.

❑ **In-line skating** Without needing to skate at high speeds, this provides a similar level of aerobic activity as running; it also works muscles in the thighs, lower back, arms and shoulders. In addition, it is considered to have 50 per cent less impact on ankle and knee joints than running.

❑ **Swimming** This is another low-impact activity and one that will improve cardiovascular fitness, muscle strength and endurance.

❑ **Water aerobics** This is also an easy exercise on the joints, and combines a cardiovascular workout with muscle toning.

❑ **Line dancing** This activity improves cardiovascular fitness and muscle tone, as well as coordination.

Enjoy your fitness training!
Believe it or not, increasing your fitness can actually be enjoyable if you approach it the right way – if jogging, skipping, cycling, joining a fitness class or sessions in the gym hold little appeal for you, there are many other activities to choose from which can be fun. While racket sports tend to increase one-sidedness, there are plenty of others that may be considered.

TIP

Choose activities you are most likely to enjoy and you will find that getting fitter is not such a chore. Once you begin to feel the benefits, you'll be more likely to keep it up. Teaming up with friends can also be a good way of keeping going on those occasions when your enthusiasm starts to flag, and can turn a fitness session into a social occasion as well.

Lunge lessons

Lunge lessons are of value to all riders, whether they are total beginners or very experienced, offering the unparalleled opportunity to work on position without having to worry about controlling the horse at the same time. A systematic course of lunge lessons is the most efficient way of teaching the rider correct balance and efficient body use. Pupils at the Spanish Riding School have daily lunge lessons for the first three years, with the initial six months of that period spent exclusively riding on the lunge.

This sort of intense frequency of lungeing is neither available, affordable or even appropriate for most riders, but if the possibility of having even occasional lunge lessons arises, it is definitely something of which to take advantage, and is one of the best investments you can make. Better still, a regular weekly lunge lesson over a period of time can do wonders for your riding, while a concentrated course of one to two dozen lessons will give a complete beginner a terrific start to their riding career.

Lunge lessons must be of good quality, however, in order for them to have value; little will be gained unless the horse used is suitable for the work, and the person teaching is knowledgeable, and competent in their handling of the horse. Any horse used for lunge lessons should fulfil certain criteria.

❏ He needs to be specifically trained for the job.
❏ He should be a known quantity: in all situations he should be sensible, steady and reliable in temperament, with regular, comfortable gaits, and fit enough to be able to sustain work at slow speeds for long periods while remaining in good balance.
❏ If the rider needs to keep their stirrups and reins in order to keep control of him, then the horse is not suitable for lunge work. Apart from the safety issues, being aware of this will, understandably, distract the attention of the rider and possibly cause concern and tension. It will also limit the exercises that can be done.
❏ For more advanced riders, the horse will ideally possess these same qualities in canter as well as in walk and trot, and in addition be able to work through more advanced transitions and gait variants.

Lunge lessons should be 30 minutes in duration with a maximum of 45 minutes, as it is tiring for the horse to work actively and well while remaining continuously on a circle. The rider will also often find – usually on dismounting – that he has been working much harder than he realized while on the lunge, so it is sensible to keep to such time limits. Most of the mounted exercises described in this book can be performed while being lunged; the knowledge and observational skills of the teacher will determine which ones are most appropriate for the pupil to perform.

USING THE EXERCISES

'There is no such thing as a standard lesson or programme; every horse and rider are different, and so no two lessons can ever be the same.'

Charles Harris 1915–2002: British equestrian scholar, teacher and author

CONTENTS

The aim of the exercises

Doing the exercises

The effect of the exercises

Some of the following 101 exercises aim to develop suppleness and flexibility, others are to improve balance and coordination, to promote independent use of the limbs, reduce tension, strengthen muscles and increase confidence. They are most often used to improve general posture and to overcome specific postural problems, but that's not where their usefulness ends. Just as you spend time warming up and working in your horse before beginning more serious work with him, doing some stretching and suppling exercises yourself at the beginning of a session can help to ease any stiffness and tension, making it possible for you to settle more quickly into a correct position. For children, exercises can also be a way of incorporating an element of fun into lessons.

Not all exercises need to be performed while in the saddle. Dismounted exercises can be just as valuable in remedying postural problems and are a good way of keeping yourself ticking over in between riding sessions, so you can continue to progress even if you can't spend as much time riding as you'd like. They can also form part of a pre-riding warm-up.

The aim of the exercises

Some exercises are quite active, others less so, but the ultimate aim is the same: that of creating a correct, integrated and balanced position. Therefore, try to think of how one part relates to another, rather than viewing the body merely as a series of bits. One thing can lead to another: for example, pushing your heels too deep can result in the lower leg being too far forward and your seat shifting backwards in the saddle, which then leads to the upper body collapsing and reliance on the reins for support. Thus the knock-on effect from one particular problem can be considerable, affecting the whole of the body, and the same can just as equally apply when it comes to making corrections. Change one thing in one area and you'll most likely need to make some kind of adjustment elsewhere, too.

The troubleshooting tips at the back of the book will help you to identify related key problem areas, but it's also useful to maintain an image in your mind of the overall ideal you are trying to achieve so you do not end up over-correcting and distorting your posture further.

When riding without reins, knot them so there is no danger of the horse getting a front foot caught up in them. It also ensures they are out of the rider's way and, in the event of an emergency, easy for the rider to pick up again.

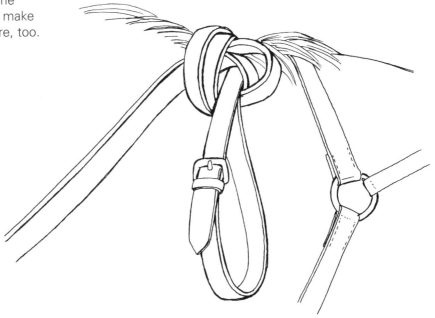

SAFETY FIRST!

Safety when performing any of the exercises is essential.

❑ Always do them in a safe, enclosed area such as a manège.
❑ Some horses may be alarmed by those exercises involving considerable rider movement. If unsure of what your horse's reaction may be, introduce them in halt with someone holding him so you can gauge his response. If necessary, borrow a steadier horse that isn't concerned by your movements.
❑ Exercises that involve riding without reins should only be performed while the horse is being held, led or lunged.
❑ Most of the exercises can be done in halt, walk or trot, as indicated in the text – but don't go faster than you feel confident and happy about.
❑ When riding an exercise that does not require stirrups, cross them in front of the saddle, placing the irons on the horse's shoulders, as described on page 22. This prevents the stirrup leathers and irons from flapping and potentially startling your horse.

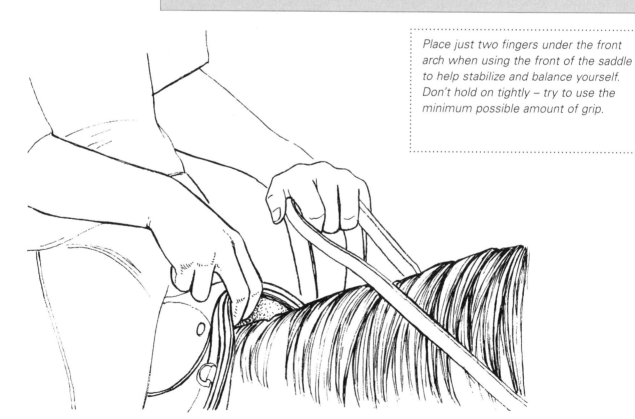

Place just two fingers under the front arch when using the front of the saddle to help stabilize and balance yourself. Don't hold on tightly – try to use the minimum possible amount of grip.

Doing the exercises

Most benefit will be gained from the exercises if they are executed according to certain criteria.

❏ Always remain within a comfortable range of movement – nothing is gained by over-exaggerating exercises, and doing so can lead to cramping, strain and injury.

❏ You should perform the exercises correctly on both reins.

❏ Do the exercises slowly, as this will allow you to stretch more fully and is less likely to lead to injury or loss of balance. It is also less likely to alarm the horse and leads to greater body self-awareness.

❏ Remember to breathe; holding your breath because you are concentrating is commonly done, but will make it more difficult to do the exercises correctly.

❏ Rest briefly between each exercise so that you have time to think about the corrections you have made and the new sensations you'll feel.

❏ Five repetitions of each exercise should be sufficient in most instances, unless otherwise stated. Do not repeat any exercise to the point where you begin to feel real discomfort or fatigue, as this in itself will lead to loss of concentration as well as incorrect and insecure posture. Having made a positional correction through use of an exercise, try to maintain the new posture, although not by stiffening or bracing yourself because this will be counter productive. If necessary, you can always repeat the exercise again whenever you feel in danger of losing the new posture.

❏ Feeling a slight stretch in your muscles is good and lets you know you have been working them, but don't push your body beyond this point and if it actually hurts, don't continue.

❏ Should you have any known health problems seek medical advice before attempting any of the exercises.

❏ You may find some exercises easier to do on one rein, or with one side of your body than the other; try to duplicate on the 'easy' side only the same range of movement that can be achieved on the 'difficult' side in order to try and avoid over-developing even further one side more than the other.

A NOTE FOR TEACHERS

If you are a teacher try all the exercises yourself before asking your pupils to do them. This will give you a better idea of their effect and also an appreciation of the demands each makes, enabling you to use them selectively and correctly according to the abilities and difficulties experienced by each individual.

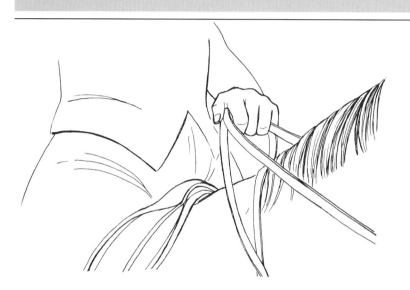

Choose those exercises that seem most applicable to you personally, and which you find of most help. In a couple of instances some exercises achieve similar effects to each other but are done differently, and you may need to try both to find which one suits you best. Remember that on a daily basis, and also as your riding ability advances, the exercises that you'll find of most benefit may change.

Only hold the reins in one hand if you are confident in your ability to control your horse while doing so.

TIP

Even if you have a specific problem area, of which you are aware, always start each riding session with a check on your seat, as this is the foundation of the rest of your posture; if it is not correct, nothing else can be either. Check next on your torso and upper body, as correctness here is essential in maintaining your seat and making it possible to make any needed adjustments to the legs and feet.

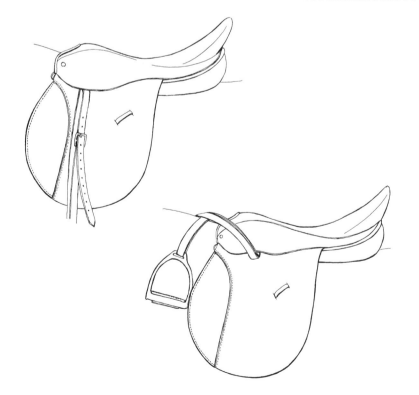

When riding without stirrups, cross the irons over in front of the saddle so they lie on the horse's shoulders. Cross the right iron over first, so that if you dismount and need to remount again, it's quick and easy to bring the near-side stirrup back over. Some leathers are adjusted by means of a buckle just above the iron in order to reduce bulk beneath the rider's thigh, but if you are using the more traditional type of leather, pull the buckle away from the stirrup bar first before crossing the irons over so you don't have an uncomfortable lump pressing into your leg.

The effect of the exercises

Finally, remember that stretching muscles and improving your posture takes time, determination and self-discipline. Sometimes you may find there's an immediate and very noticeable difference – maybe you feel more comfortable, or find it easier to do something, or observe that your horse is working better – and this can help motivate you to keep working at it. But very often the differences, although noticeable, are less dramatic, and sometimes the new posture can feel odd initially. This is when you must be prepared to persevere; there are no shortcuts, and the more ingrained a postural habit is, the harder it is to change it.

Looking on the brighter side, however, this also applies to good posture, in that once acquired and established, the easier and more effortless it is to maintain. Don't expect the impossible. Change things little by little, and gradually your position will improve. Then you'll be able to reap the rewards of a more mutually harmonious, successful and satisfying partnership with every horse you ride.

Either a breastplate or neckstrap can be useful to hold on to in an emergency, rather than pulling on the horse's mouth.

THE IDEAL POSITION

'In training horses, one trains oneself as well.'

Antoine de Pluvinel 1552-1620: French riding master, teacher and author

THE EXERCISES

01. Flatwork position

02. Jumping Position

Working on your position shouldn't be something to which you only pay attention during lessons or schooling sessions; it should be an automatic habit at all times when mounted, so that it becomes second nature to continually monitor your position and your actions as well as their effect on your horse.

Posture isn't a static thing, but alters subtly each second with the movement and direction of the horse, and balance and suppleness make a vital contribution to your ability to maintain it. Although to an onlooker you may appear to be sitting still, in reality there is continuous movement, with constant minute adjustments taking place in your muscles, joints and weight distribution, which enable you to maintain a correct posture and to absorb fully the movement of the horse. After trying Exercise 1, repeat the first three steps again with your eyes shut and you'll notice that even remaining motionless requires a degree of suppleness, coordination and frequent small corrections to your balance.

The influence of gait speed

As gait speed increases, so maintaining a good posture becomes more challenging. Furthermore it becomes even more difficult if you are riding an unbalanced, stiff or unschooled horse. With these horses, it is essential that your position is as good as possible if you are going to have any success in improving them, so you will need to be especially vigilant in checking yourself. (See Chapter 1, The ideal position, page 10.)

Fast work

The flatwork posture is modified when cantering, galloping across country or jumping. While riding at speed, the stirrups are shortened to make it easier for the rider to adopt either a light, forward seat or to raise it slightly out of the saddle, with the upper body inclined slightly forwards. This helps free the horse's back and enables the rider to keep his weight balanced over the horse's centre of gravity. The shorter stirrup length also provides a greater degree of security in the event of the horse stumbling – although on the minus side it does fix the rider's leg to a degree, thus limiting its action and effect.

Jumping position

When you are jumping, the 'riding at speed' position is simply exaggerated a little more.

❏ As the horse takes off the rider begins to fold forwards from the hips, keeping the back flat and looking ahead; the larger the fence, the more the rider will need to fold forwards in order to remain in balance with the horse.

❏ The flexion of the hip, knee and ankle joints increases, enabling them to work better as shock absorbers. The rider's weight is carried mainly by the thigh, knee and heel.

❏ The knee should be in close contact with the saddle.

❏ The heel should always be the lowest point of the rider's body, slightly lower than the toe.

❏ As the horse's head and neck stretch forwards, the arms and hands move forwards towards his mouth so that a soft rein contact is kept but without causing any restriction. This position is at its most exaggerated when the horse is in mid-air directly above the fence.

❏ As he begins to land on the far side, the rider's torso begins to return to a more upright posture.

Flatwork position

This posture is the ideal for flatwork on level going in a safe environment.

Benefits

You can gain a feel for the correct mounted posture while standing on the ground – this exercise is also a good way of heightening awareness of your body, and increasing your capacity for self-analysis. When you are in a correct, balanced stance it should be relatively easy and effortless to maintain it.

How to do it

❑ Stand upright, with your feet placed around 60–75cm (2–2½ft) apart and with your weight evenly distributed over them.

❑ Keeping your body vertical, slowly flex your knees until you are in a similar position as when mounted. Keep your ears, shoulders, hips and heels aligned vertically with each other.

❑ Flex your elbows so that both hands are positioned as if holding the reins.

❑ Experiment a little, holding one hand higher than the other, for example, with the head tilted, or your upper body leaning forwards, backwards or to one side. Move into these incorrect positions slowly, noting in what ways moving one part affects everything else, and how it feels, before returning to a correct posture. This helps you to understand how each part of your body relates to the rest, so that, armed with this knowledge, you are better able to make the right positional corrections.

DO: practise in front of a full-length mirror if one is available, as this is a good way of checking as to whether your perception of what your body is doing matches the reality. Observe yourself both from the front and in profile.

AVOID: holding your breath while concentrating, as this will make you stiff, and reduces your ability to feel what your body is doing.

Jumping position

As well as your flatwork position, you can also practise your jumping position while you are dismounted.

Benefits

This is a useful preparatory exercise for novices who haven't done any jumping before, and can also be of benefit to more advanced riders who have acquired bad habits, particularly standing up in the stirrups. Make your movements slow and steady so you can really think about your balance and coordination.

How to do it

❏ Start as in Exercise 1, with your feet placed comfortably apart at shoulder width, knees slightly flexed and hands holding imaginary reins.

❏ Keeping both heels flat to the floor, fold your upper body forwards from the hips while sliding your seat out behind you so it acts as a counterbalance. Notice how the flexion simultaneously increases in your knee and ankle joints as you move into the jumping position.

❏ At the same time, allow both hands to move forwards away from your body; think of the elbows pushing the wrists.

❏ Slowly return to your starting position.

Moving on

Once you've got the feel for the correct position, try it while standing on a pole, making sure the balls of your feet are on it. This allows you to drop your heel slightly deeper, and to check that you really are in balance – as much of your weight should be carried behind as in front of a vertical line drawn upwards from the pole. If you haven't got it quite right, you'll find that the pole rolls and you have to step off it.

DO: keep your back flat.

AVOID: looking down as your upper body folds forwards – keep looking straight ahead. If you look down, your shoulders tend to round, your ribcage collapses and your upper body becomes out of balance so it is harder to recover and return to your starting position.

THE SEAT

'Seen from the side, the rider appears to sit in the middle of the horse, with as much of the horse in front of him as behind him.'

Hans von Heydebreck: early 20th-century German teacher, competitor, judge and dressage authority

THE EXERCISES

03. Jockey seat

04. Heel turn

Developing a 'good seat' is crucial to your stability, balance, your ability to communicate effectively and to absorb the horse's movement. It forms the base of support, and when correctly positioned with the head, neck and upper body aligned above, this produces a very secure, almost adhesive effect. If the seat is incorrect, however, everything else will be too, so it should be the first part of your body that you check when you mount and check your position before moving off. If you have a problem with any other part of your body, always ensure that your seat is correct before working more specifically on exercises to help the problem area.

The word 'seat' is applied loosely in riding and is taken to mean that area encompassing the waist to the knees.

Learning to sit correctly

As much as possible of the seat – including the upper part of the thigh as well as the buttocks – should be in contact with the saddle, with the rider's two seatbones positioned in the lowest and most central part of the saddle. Before mounting, get a feel for where your seatbones are by sitting on a wooden chair or bench. 'Walk' your seat forwards until you are near the edge – you will become aware of your seatbones as you shuffle your seat forwards on the hard surface of the chair. Then place your hands beneath your seat, and sit as tall as possible by raising (not pushing forwards) your breastbone. You will now be able to feel your seatbones pressing against your fingers. Rock slightly forwards and you should feel the pressure lessening the further forwards you go; then rock slightly backwards and it should become firmer, with the feeling of giving a forceful forwards 'push'.

Notice what happens in the rest of your body at the same time – as you tilt the pelvis forwards your lower back becomes more hollow and stiff, and as you tilt it backwards your ribcage becomes slumped and muscular tension in the thighs increases. Your seat should be midway between these two extremes, with the pelvis in a vertical 'neutral' position. When mounted, try to duplicate the same feel; Exercise 3 Jockey seat may help you in doing this.

A deep seat

'Sitting deeply' is a frequently used phrase, but one which often seems to have an adverse effect on the rider's position.

Rather than trying to push the seat down or grind it into the saddle, it's more a case of being able to relax the muscles of the upper thigh and those round the hip sufficiently to allow the seat to make the fullest possible contact. Then allow gravity to assist you. At the same time you need to think of your torso, from just above the hips, floating up and slightly forwards with the movement of the horse. Riding without stirrups, particularly in trot, has traditionally been used as a way of helping to develop a deeper seat, but can have the opposite effect if done to excess and without sufficient regard as to what the back and legs are doing. While it can heighten your awareness of your seatbones, it is an exercise that is just as much about balance and correctly absorbing the horse's movement, and is dealt with in Chapter 6, The upper body.

HELPFUL EXERCISES

The exercise ball exercises in Chapter 13 (64 Gym ball) and in Chapter 17 (80 Stomach toner) are also good practice for helping to find a neutral pelvis – if you are not correctly positioned you will find it difficult to balance and will be inclined to stiffen to compensate.

In addition to the exercises here, you will find the leg exercises in Chapter 10 of benefit, as tight muscles will prevent you from being able to sit correctly; also Exercise 44 (Toe straightener) from Chapter 11. As the lumbar (lower back) vertebrae also play an essential part in maintaining and using the seat. You may also find it helpful to refer to Chapter 6.

Jockey seat

This exercise will show you how to sit in closer contact with the saddle.

Benefits

This exercise helps you to locate your seatbones while mounted. It also helps to stretch the muscles in the upper thigh area, making it easier to open your seat and to sit in closer contact with the saddle. It can be a useful exercise to do after mounting, but only if your horse is steady and being held.

How to do it

❏ Ask your horse to stand as squarely as possible and then place both the reins in one hand. Take hold of the front of the saddle with the other hand to help you keep your balance.

❏ Raise both knees up until they are almost touching over the withers in front of the saddle, jockey style. You should be able to distinctly feel your seatbones resting on the saddle. If necessary, slowly 'walk' them forwards until they are in the central, lowest part of the saddle; you may need someone to help you check on this from the side. Check that your weight is evenly distributed across both seatbones.

❏ Slowly stretch both legs out very slightly to the side and lower them back and down around your horse's sides, keeping control of the movement rather than letting your legs drop abruptly. Avoid trying to lift the legs too far outwards or it may cause you to tip on to the front of your seat. Should you overdo things you may also feel pain in the hip joint or find the muscles cramping painfully. This might happen inadvertently, in which case you should bring the affected leg up and forwards over the front of the saddle to relieve the discomfort.

❏ Ask your assistant to check that your pelvis is in a vertical neutral position and your upper body is upright before you move off.

DO: try and keep your back straight and vertical – try not to hunch or curl up, or lean backwards.

AVOID: lifting your shoulders or tightening through your jaw. It can be a good idea to follow this exercise with some head, neck (Chapter 5) and shoulder exercises (Chapter 7) in order to help get rid of any excess tension.

Heel turn

Practise stretching the thigh and hip muscles in this way and you will develop a deeper, more secure seat.

Benefits

This exercise helps stretch the muscles at the top of the thigh and around the hip, allowing the seat to come into a deeper, closer contact with the saddle. It is also a beneficial exercise for those who tend to grip inwards and upwards with the back of the legs and heels.

How to do it

❏ While your horse is in halt, place the reins in one hand and hold the front of the saddle with the other to help you maintain your balance.

❏ Lift your right leg outwards away from your horse's side, so that it just comes out of contact with the saddle. Turn the heel slightly outwards and then slowly and gently allow the leg to come back into contact with the horse's sides, drawing the knee back and downwards a little as you do so.

❏ Repeat with your left leg.

DO: keep looking up and ahead; increase your familiarity with your body by *feeling* what you are doing, rather than trying to see – which is also likely to make you crooked. Do try to keep your upper body vertical, too – you should avoid curling forwards or leaning backwards.

AVOID: trying to lift your leg or turn your heel to the point where you feel pain in your hip joint. If you get a cramp, bring the affected leg up and forwards over the front of the saddle to relieve the discomfort.

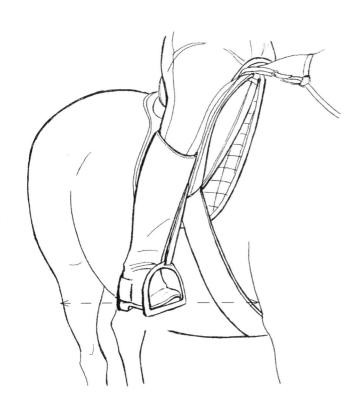

THE HEAD AND NECK

'… the rider's mind must also work perpetually, in order to detect all kinds of opportunities to arrive at his goals, without letting any movement pass unnoticed, nor any opportunity unused.'

Antoine de Pluvinel 1552–1620: French riding master, teacher and author

The head is a surprisingly heavy part of the anatomy, weighing on average between 3.5–4.7kg (8–10.25lb), and your riding hat adds a further half kilogram (1lb). Thanks to your neck, your head has a fairly wide range of movement and taking this into account, plus its weight and the fact that it is at the top of your body, it can exert a considerable influence, for better or worse, on the rest of your body and posture.

Head roll

This exercise will help to release tension through the neck and jaw.

Benefits

The head roll is good for helping to release tension through the sides and back of the neck, and to encourage a feeling of lengthening through the back of the neck if you have a tendency to poke your chin forwards. The act of dropping your head forwards also makes it hard to clench your teeth, so it's good for helping to get rid of any tightness around the jaw, too.

How to do it

❏ First, ask your horse to come to a halt. Then very slowly allow your head to drop forwards slightly.

❏ Keeping your chin central, slowly roll your head to the left and then to the right. It should feel as though the crown of your head is describing a very shallow half circle. Full circular movements should be avoided.

❏ Some people find it easier to relax and benefit more from this exercise by doing it with their eyes shut, but if you want to try this, make sure the horse is being held. Repeat five times.

DO: stay within a comfortable range of movement, and make the rolling movement as steady and slow as you possibly can.

AVOID: keeping going if you start to feel giddy or disoriented. Stop, and only try again when you feel better, but this time with your eyes shut. Avoid slumping through the ribcage while you are doing the exercise.

EXERCISE 6

Lemon-sucking

Soft chewing movements, as if sucking a lemon, will help to relax tense jaw muscles.

Benefits

This is a very simple exercise and requires only a reasonable amount of imagination. It can be useful during those moments when anxiety makes your mouth feel dry or you find it hard to swallow, because it encourages salivation while helping to relax tense, clenched jaw muscles and, to a lesser extent, those of the neck.

How to do it

❏ Pretend that you are sucking on a slice of lemon.
❏ Allow your imagination to do the rest! You'll be surprised at how effective a response this produces.

DO: try making small, soft chewing movements with your mouth to help keep the jaw area relaxed.

AVOID: riding while you are eating or chewing food in case you bite your tongue or choke.

Infinity and beyond

Tension in the neck will often lead to tension in the shoulders and this exercise will help to resolve both.

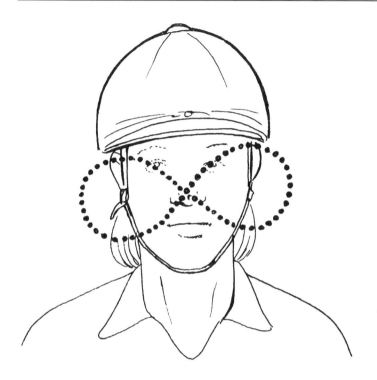

Benefits

This exercise helps release tension in the neck and jaw, especially if you are feeling stressed. This can also aid in relaxing the shoulders, as tension in the neck is often present in the shoulders too.

How to do it

❏ Ask your horse to halt. Allow your head to gently tilt forward slightly.
❏ Use the tip of your nose to slowly draw a figure of infinity sign in the air (this looks like a slightly flattened and elongated figure-of-eight that is lying on its side).
❏ Repeat five times in one direction and then five times in the other direction. You will probably find it easier one way than the other.

DO: stop if you begin to feel dizzy or disoriented. Wait until you feel better and then try again with closed eyes, making sure your horse is held.

AVOID: making the loops too large or allowing the ribcage to slump while doing the exercise.

EXERCISE

8

Chin tuck

Stop yourself jutting your chin out with this exercise and thereby release any tension you might feel in your neck, head and jaw.

Benefits
Try this exercise if you become aware of sticking your chin out or pushing your head forwards. It will help to restore a more correct headcarriage and encourage you to gently stretch through the back of the neck instead of hollowing it.

How to do it
❑ Ask your horse to halt.
❑ Place the reins in one hand and place the tip of the index finger of the other hand on the point of the chin.
❑ Gently push the chin in a backwards and slightly downwards direction with the finger tip, until you begin to feel the lower jaw relax. At the same time the crown of your head should begin to feel as though it is moving in a forward and upward direction.

DO: try following this exercise with Exercise 9 Head stretch; if you ask someone to hold your horse so that both your hands are free, you can even combine them for greater effect, placing one index finger on your chin and the other on the crown of your head.

AVOID: exaggerating the posture to the point where your chin becomes buried in the front of your chest – this is a subtle exercise and it should be carried out slowly and carefully.

TIP
If you need to look down to check on trotting diagonals or canter leads, try to use peripheral vision instead of actually tilting your head forwards.

Head stretch

In this exercise the whole of the torso stretches, and as your head and neck posture improves you will feel lighter and better balanced.

Benefits

When reminding yourself to look up, it's important to do it the right way. If you just raise your chin and tilt your head, you will end up hollowing the back of the neck, which will then cause tension in the shoulders and make it almost impossible to sit up properly through the torso. This exercise helps remind you of the role that your neck plays in correct headcarriage, as well as to improve it.

How to do it

❏ Ask your horse to halt. Place both reins in one hand.
❏ Place the tip of the index finger of your other hand on the crown of your head.
❏ Now think about lengthening up through the back of your neck as if you were trying to touch the fingertip with the top of your head.

DO: note the way in which the whole of your torso simultaneously stretches, feeling lighter and better balanced as your head and neck posture improves. Try to maintain this when you take up the reins again with both hands.

AVOID: pressing down with your index finger – remember the point is to try and stretch up towards it!

EXERCISE 10

Up and away

This exercise helps you stay straight as you jump, and to maintain impulsion as you land and ride away from a fence.

Benefits

Looking up and ahead is especially important when jumping. It is vital in helping to recover balance and impulsion on landing after a fence, and ensures that the rider is thinking about, and ready to ride towards, the next fence.

How to do it

❏ When jumping, ask someone to stand at a safe distance beyond a fence, with one arm held up in the air, the hand made into a fist.

❏ As you approach the fence, your assistant holds up one, two, three, four or all five fingers; keep looking at the raised hand and call out the number of fingers being shown.

❏ This can also help with straightness, provided the person on the ground is standing in a line with the centre of the fence and not to one side of it.

THE UPPER BODY

6

'The light and steady hand depends on the light and steady position of the upper body.'

Gustav Steinbrecht 1808–1885: German riding master, teacher and author on classical horsemanship

THE EXERCISES

11. Hands on

12. Riding without stirrups

13. Hands in the air

14. Helicopter

15. Bracing the back

16. Back to back

17. Back push

18. Back stretch

Correct alignment of the upper body helps to stabilize the seat and makes it possible to apply effective leg aids. Suppleness in the lower back absorbs the horse's movement, together with the thighs and buttocks, and allows the upper body to appear still so that rein aids can be applied independently and precisely. The lower back also plays an important part in the application of the seat aids.

Ideally the upper body should be vertical, with the shoulders directly above the hip joints, but there are exceptions to this. In rising trot it may be inclined forwards slightly to facilitate the movement, and a little more so when tackling gradients, riding across country, galloping and jumping in order to remain in a good balance with the horse.

ABSORBING THE HORSE'S MOVEMENT

Before you can begin to learn how to influence the horse with your seat and back, you must first learn how to sit passively and absorb the movement. Although you should appear to an onlooker to be sitting still, this lack of motion is in relation to the horse which is in movement, not the ground, which is static. The movement of the horse's back should be absorbed through the lower back, buttocks and thighs, and also involves the hip, knee and ankle joints working as shock absorbers. Try to relax and go with the movement, remembering that as well as up/down movement there will also be backward/forward and side-to-side movement. Attempting to lock yourself down into the saddle will make you stiff, causing the horse to brace himself protectively against you. It will also make it even more difficult for you to sit in close contact with the saddle and apply the leg aids effectively.

The importance of strong abdominal muscles

Although you don't need to sport a well defined 'six pack', strong abdominal muscles are needed to help stabilize the spine and midsection. If they are weak you will tend to compensate by tightening your arms, shoulders and legs, which will not only affect your ability to communicate with your horse, but will restrict his movement too.
If you feel you are weak in this area, some of the exercises in this section will help you address this; you will also find others that will help in Chapter 17 Dismounted exercises.

Hands on

This exercise will help you to be more supple in the lower back and move with the movement of the horse.

Benefits

This exercise is very simple and can help you in learning how to absorb the horse's movement through your seat and lower back. Do not attempt it if it is difficult to control your horse with the reins held in one hand; ask someone to lead you instead. If you have a tendency to hollow your back and stiffen, try Exercise 17 Back push instead.

How to do it

❏ Place the reins in your outside hand. Place the other hand, palm facing outwards, in the small of your back.
❏ This should increase your awareness of any tension and stiffness in this area and will help you to focus on allowing your lower back to relax and move with the movement of the horse. Experiment with the height of your hand, moving it lower down, so that you cover all of the lumbar vertebrae.

DO: try an alternative position, too, cupping your inside hand over the top of your inside hip. If you are being led or lunged, you can dispense with the reins altogether and place a hand on each hip.

AVOID: trying to exaggerate the movement of your lower back and seat.

TIP
If you are being led or lunged so that both of your hands are free, try placing the back of your inside hand in the small of your back as before and the palm of your outside hand immediately opposite, on your abdomen. This can be helpful for those riders who tend to 'wiggle' in the area, rather than correctly absorbing the movement down through the thighs and upwards through the seat and spinal column. Try it when riding upward transitions too, to encourage good upper body posture and leg aids, rather than pushing the seat back and forth.

Riding without stirrups

In moderation, sitting to the trot without stirrups helps to deepen the seat and improve balance and thereby also helps to reduce tension.

Benefits

Provided it is done sensibly, sitting to the trot without stirrups can help deepen the seat and improve balance, and also improve the rider's ability to absorb the movement of the horse's back. See also Chapter 10, Exercise 37 Sitting to the trot with stirrups p. 94.

How to do it

❏ Cross both stirrups over the saddle in front of you. Ask your horse to move forwards from walk into trot, beginning with just a slow jog, as this will be easier to sit to. Try not to tense through the buttocks or thighs, because any tension will reduce their ability to absorb the movement.

❏ Allow gravity to draw your legs downwards, but think of your torso simultaneously lengthening upwards from the hips – the lower back is a key area for absorbing the movement and if you slouch or collapse it will prevent this from happening. Allow your legs to hang naturally, with the toes dropping, as this will help you to relax the thigh muscles. Check that you do not grip up with the knees, the back of the heels or the thighs. After a while raise your toes so that your feet are in the correct riding position with your heels lower than your toes.

❏ Increase the horse's activity gradually and only by as much as you are able to cope with – increasing his activity will also increase the amount of movement in his back.

DO: place the reins in one hand and use the other to hold the front of the saddle to help stabilize yourself if necessary.

AVOID: persevering with sitting to the trot for long periods if you are not comfortable – there's no benefit to be gained by the rider adopting a 'no pain, no gain' attitude. Once tired, uncomfortable or losing your balance, things will only get worse and can also cause damage to the horse's back. Sit for only a few strides of trot at a time and the moment either you or the horse begins to feel uncomfortable, return to walk. With practice you'll find that you can sit comfortably and easily for progressively more and more successive strides at a time.

Moving on

After working without stirrups for a while, you may feel that when you're ready to take them back, you're able to lengthen them – but take care to do this gradually. To begin with let them down by just one hole rather than two or three (see Chapter 10, Stirrup length p. 93).

Hands in the air

Stretching upwards will encourage better posture and teach the rider not to collapse the upper body.

Benefits

This exercise encourages good stretching up through the front of the ribcage, so is ideal for riders who tend to collapse or slump through the ribcage.

How to do it

❑ While your horse is being led or lunged, knot the reins and lay them on his neck.

❑ Raise both hands up in the air above you; keep your fingers lightly pressed together while trying to see how much you can stretch the fingertips upwards.

DO: keep both arms vertical and allow the feeling of lengthening to travel up through the ribcage evenly. Ask the person on the ground to check if your hands are level with each other – if not, it may be because you are sitting crookedly.

AVOID: collapsing through one side of your waist. If this happens, lifting up the hand on that side only will help considerably in preventing this from occurring; think about stretching downwards through the thigh on the same side too.

TIP
If you have no one to help you and can safely control your horse holding the reins in one hand, raising just a single hand up in the air will also help encourage better posture.

Helicopter

Stability and straightness will be helped by this exercise as well as balance and suppleness.

Benefits

This exercise helps improve balance as well as increasing suppleness through the waist area. It will also show up any crookedness – one arm will be lower than the other if this is the case.

How to do it

❏ While someone leads or lunges your horse, knot the reins and lay them on the horse's neck. Spread both arms out, so they are just below shoulder height on each side.

❏ Keeping both arms in line with each other, first slowly rotate clockwise and then anti-clockwise. Turn only as far as you are able without twisting your hips and without either of your seatbones leaving the saddle.

DO: allow your legs to stretch down the horse's sides to help you maintain stability and straightness.

AVOID: looking downwards or projecting your head and neck forwards.

Bracing the back

You can learn how to apply back and seat aids correctly by practising various degrees of 'bracing' the back on an exercise ball first and, having got the feel of it, then try doing it on a horse.

Benefits

'Bracing' the back should be a feeling of firming up the movement in the lower back, rather than becoming locked, rigid, or leaning backwards; the rider should remain harmoniously in balance with the horse throughout. You can practise varying degrees of 'bracing' the back on an exercise ball first and, having got the feel of it, then on a horse.

How to do it

❏ Sit on the centre of an exercise ball, both feet flat on the floor and shoulder width apart and with the knees in line above your ankles. Keep your upper body vertical with your shoulders above your hips and looking ahead.

❏ Place each hand, palm down, on the top of each thigh and then gently but firmly press down.

❏ Next, put both arms behind your back, cupping each elbow with the opposite hand, and push gently into the small of the back.

❏ Try both of these different 'feels' on a horse while being led or lunged. Do not maintain a constant 'bracing' action, but apply it as you would any aid – asking, releasing and then waiting to see how your horse responds. This may vary from one individual to another, depending on his level of education.

DO: breathe normally.

AVOID: leaning backwards or stiffening through the lower back.

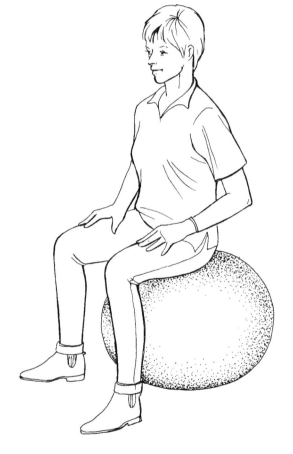

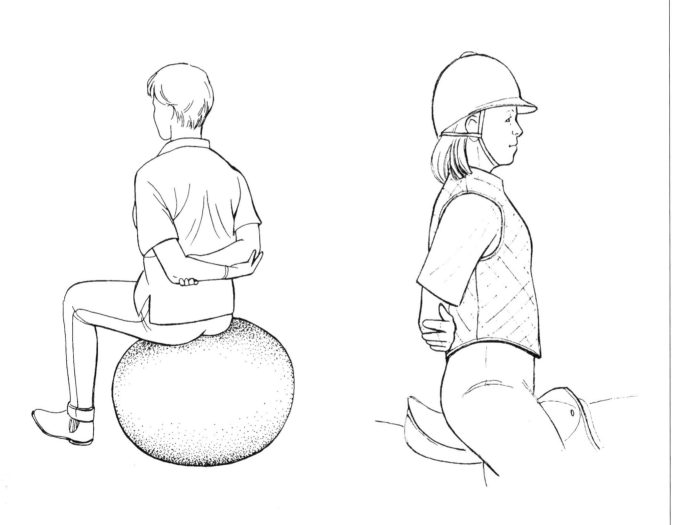

Back to back

This exercise will help the rider to 'sit tall' without being stiff and can be especially helpful for those who hollow through the lower back.

Benefits

This dismounted exercise helps free up tensions in the lumbar and pelvic regions. As well as being beneficial for riders tight in these areas or who tend to hollow their back, it generally helps you to 'sit tall' in the saddle without stiffening. Team up with a friend so you can help each other.

How to do it

❏ Lie down with your knees flexed and your feet flat on the floor.
❏ Check how much space there is between the ground and the small of your back by slipping one hand beneath, then rest both arms by your sides.
❏ Your friend then takes hold of the ankle and calf of one of your legs so it is fully supported and very slowly, gently and smoothly draws it away from you, whilst keeping the lower leg horizontal to the ground.
❏ This gentle traction is maintained for a count of three and then just as slowly, gently and smoothly it is released, and the foot placed back on the floor.

DO: repeat with the other leg and then check the gap between the small of the back and the ground again – it should now be less.

AVOID: jerking, pulling strongly, twisting the foot, or moving the leg to the side – keep it in line with the hip bone.

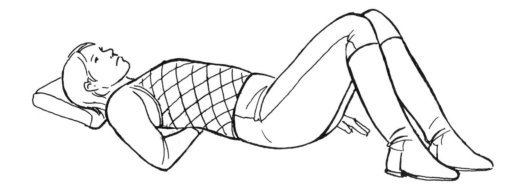

Back push

This exercise will help those riders who are tense in their lower back, causing it to become hollow.

Benefits

This can be a subtle but effective exercise for those who tend to hollow their back. Only try it if you can safely control your horse holding the reins in one hand; otherwise ask someone to lead you.

How to do it

- ❏ Place reins in your outside hand, and then place the back of your inside hand against the small of your back, palm facing away from you.
- ❏ Push the back of your hand firmly against your back for a count of three.
- ❏ Very slowly, begin to release the pressure of your hand, allowing your back to follow its movement as though glued to it.

DO: check that your seat is correctly positioned in the saddle.

AVOID: riding with stirrups that are too long, because this can cause you to hollow your back.

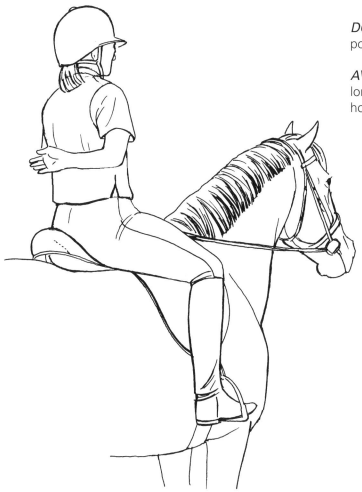

Back stretch

Practise sitting tall by stretching upwards through the front of the body, raising the breastbone and becoming 'wider' across the chest.

Benefits

This exercise can be beneficial for riders who tend to slump – it also encourages the shoulders to lower and stretch open. Only try it if you can safely control your horse when riding with the reins in one hand; otherwise you should ask someone to lead you.

How to do it

❑ Place both reins in your outside hand.
❑ Place your open right hand behind your back, knuckles towards you and palm facing outwards. Slide your hand upwards as far as you comfortably can, towards your shoulder blades.

DO: check you are not sitting on the back of your seat, because this can cause a slumped ribcage.

AVOID: exaggerating this exercise or it could lead to hollowing of the back. Also try Exercise 13 Hands in the air to see which one is most beneficial for you personally.

TIP

Trying to sit taller without thinking about how you are doing it can make you ramrod straight but also ramrod stiff – and maybe with raised, tight shoulders as well. Improve your upper body posture by stretching upwards through the front of the body, raising your breastbone and stretching open across your chest.

THE SHOULDERS

'Horse and rider are in perfect union, they form a delicately balanced whole, a living work of art ...'

Hans von Heydebreck: early 20th century German teacher, competitor, judge and dressage authority

The shoulders should be level with each other, relaxed and parallel to the hips. While riding or schooling on the flat, they should also be positioned in line above the hips. Together with the torso, this helps to stabilize the seat, preventing it from slipping backwards or to the side. Any stiffness in the shoulders or deviation from correct alignment with the hips will not only affect the rest of the rider's posture and security, but will also directly influence the quality of the rein contact, making it difficult to make this sympathetic and elastic.

Any stiffness in the shoulders, or deviation from correct alignment will affect rider security and quality of rein contact.

Shoulder shrug

Relieve excess tension with this simple exercise and improve your whole way of sitting in the saddle.

Benefits

This is a good exercise for helping to release stiffness and tightness in the shoulders, and is a useful warm-up exercise because sometimes you may not even be aware of just how tense and stiff you are in this area, particularly if you've had a hectic or stressful day at work. By allowing the shoulders to lower, correct breathing becomes easier, a more elastic rein contact can develop and you will be inclined to sit taller and altogether more softly in the saddle.

How to do it

- ❏ First, increase the tension for a moment by tightly hunching up both shoulders under your ears. Hold for three seconds.
- ❏ Slowly allow your shoulders to roll backwards and downwards.
- ❏ Repeat two to three times.

DO: be sure to breathe out as you release your shoulders.

AVOID: pushing your chin out and forwards as you move your shoulders backwards and downwards.

TIP
Move your shoulders further apart, rather than trying to push them back. If you can imagine that you have a small egg-sized piece of foam rubber resting under each armpit, this may help you to keep your chest open and shoulders feeling wide.

Single shoulder lifts

If you feel you are tense through one hand or arm, this exercise can help to restore softness and a more elastic contact.

Benefits

The benefits of this exercise are similar as for the shoulder shrug (Exercise 19). However, some people may find it easier to work on a single shoulder at a time, in which case make sure you repeat the exercise the same number of times with each shoulder. It can also be a useful exercise to do a couple of times if you feel you are becoming a little fixed through one arm or hand, or even if you just feel an overwhelming desire to pull on one rein. Releasing tension through the shoulder will help to create a softer hand and arm and consequently a more elastic contact, to which the horse will almost always respond in a more positive way.

How to do it

❏ Slowly raise one shoulder up towards the ear on that side.
❏ As your shoulder reaches the highest point, slowly allow it to drop down again, rolling it backwards as you do so. Breathe out at the same time as this helps to release tension more effectively, allowing the shoulder to lower more.

DO: bring your shoulder up towards your ear rather than tilting your head over to that side.

AVOID: trying to bring your shoulder up as high as the ear – it's almost impossible to do so with a single shoulder without tilting the head and becoming crooked through the seat and torso.

TIP
Visualize your shoulder blades as being able to glide freely across the back of your ribcage.

Elbow push

If you have a tendency to be round-shouldered in posture, this exercise will help you to open them up, sit taller and be more elegant in the saddle. It will also make your rein contact more sympathetic.

Benefits

This exercise is extremely beneficial for those riders who are round-shouldered. It will also encourage the rider to stretch across the front of the chest and, although to a lesser extent, to stretch through the front of the ribcage.

How to do it

❏ Ask someone to hold your horse in halt. This exercise can also be done in halt or walk on the lunge.

❏ Knot and let go of the reins, letting them lie on the horse's neck.

❏ Raise both arms out in front of you at shoulder height, then flex your elbows fully until your hands are level with the top of your chest with fingertips touching.

❏ Slowly move both elbows back simultaneously, allowing the shoulder blades to glide across the back of your ribcage as you do so. Move the elbows back only as far as it is comfortable to do so. After even only a couple of repetitions you may find that your range of movement is increasing.

❏ Allow the fingertips to slowly slide together to their starting position so they touch again. Repeat five times.

DO: breathe in as the elbows move backwards and keep the forearms parallel to the ground.

AVOID: pushing your chin forwards as the elbows are pushed backwards or attempting to thrust the chest forwards, as this will cause you to hollow your back and lead to you perching on the front of your seat.

Arm circling

This exercise can help with more than one rider problem. If you have round shoulders, slump through the upper body or collapse one side of your waist, arm circling may improve your posture.

Benefits

Rounded shoulders and slumping through the upper body often go together. This exercise is useful for this combination of problems since it encourages stretching up through the front of the ribcage as well as helping to relax and open up rounded or stiff shoulders. It is also good for riders who tend to collapse through one side of the waist – circle the arm on that side.

How to do it

❏ If riding independently, place both the reins into one hand. If you are being led or lunged, the reins can either be held in one hand or knotted and left lying on the horse's neck. Do not attempt this exercise while riding independently unless you are confident in your ability to control your horse with the reins held in one hand.

❏ Slowly circle your free arm forwards, upwards and backwards until it has described a full 360 degree arc and is hanging by your side again. As the arm reaches a point just past your ear, and begins to travel backwards, the circle made should move in a slightly outwards direction away from your body otherwise the shoulder will lock and begin to rise. Try to breathe in as your arm is moving upwards and exhale again as it travels downwards.

❏ Keep the elbow and fingers very slightly flexed as this will increase the range of movement in the shoulder. Start with smaller circles, gradually making them larger as the shoulder joint feels freer and more comfortable.

❏ Repeat this exercise five times and then circle the other arm, also in an upwards and backwards direction.

DO: be sure to keep the movement slow and deliberate.

AVOID: allowing the ribcage to slump or collapse after the exercise.

23

Elbow circling

Circling the elbow backwards will effectively release tension in the shoulder joint.

Benefits

This exercise helps to open the front of the chest and reduces tension and roundness in the shoulders.

How to do it

❑ If riding independently, hold both the reins in one hand; or if being held, led or lunged, the reins can either be held in one hand, or knotted and left lying on the horse's neck.

❑ Place the fingertips of your free hand lightly on the top of the shoulder on the same side.

❑ Draw a circle in the air with the point of your elbow. Start off with a small circle about the size of a golf ball, then slowly increase it to the size of a tennis ball and then a football.

❑ Repeat ten times and then repeat with the other elbow.

DO: always circle your elbow backwards; forward circling doesn't open up the shoulder joint as effectively, will accentuate round shoulders and can lead to the upper body tipping forwards.

AVOID: tilting your head towards or away from the elbow that is making circles.

TTouch body wrap

Changing a bad habit is difficult if you aren't consciously aware of its existence, or to what degree it is present. Using a couple of elasticated bandages to form a 'body wrap' can help to highlight problems of posture.

Benefits

It may look odd, but wearing a wrap while riding helps increase your awareness of what your shoulders are doing – rounding, lifting or stiffening – and encourages you to relax and adopt a better, more relaxed posture. It can also increase self-awareness of your balance, help reduce tension in the pelvis and back, and discourage any tendency to stiffen against the movement of the horse. It can also be worn while dismounted to help you develop a feel for correct posture, since habits formed in everyday movements and activities tend to be carried through to your posture in the saddle.

How to do it

❑ Take an elasticated exercise or tail bandage and cross it over diagonally from one shoulder to just above the opposite hip.

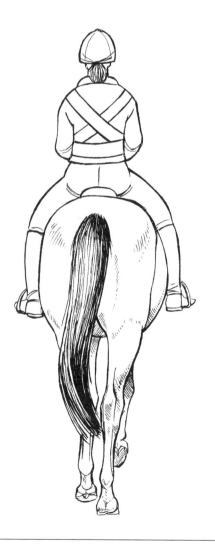

- Bring both ends back around the waist and secure with a quick release knot.
- Use a second bandage to repeat as above from the other shoulder.
- Alternatively place a bandage across the top of both shoulders, passing it behind the neck, then bring both ends in front of the shoulders and down under the arms. Cross them behind the back, bringing them back around to the front and around the waist. Finally, secure them.

DO: try the bandages in both of the ways shown; everyone's personal experience is different and you may find one way more helpful than the other. The bandages should have plenty of stretch in them so they move with your body and are less likely to slip.

AVOID: putting the bandages on too tightly; they should only be just firm enough not to slip down. The aim is to create better body awareness, not to restrict movement.

8

THE ARMS AND WRISTS

'Rider and horse must meet with joy and part as friends.'

Colonel Friedrich von Krane: 19th century Prussian cavalryman, commander and author on classical horsemanship

THE EXERCISES

The rider's leg aids energize the horse and the hand then receives what the legs have created, but the flexibility of the arm is responsible for the subtlety with which the hands receive, and in turn guide and channel this energy, and communicate with the horse. It also affects how receptive you are to feedback from the horse via the reins. Stiffness through the arms and shoulders will invariably make the horse more likely to resist the contact and try to evade the action of the bit.

As a rule we tend to rely on our arms for balance. We will almost certainly put out a hand to save ourselves from falling, and when stability is seriously compromised both arms will usually wave around quite considerably. Obviously this cannot be allowed to happen when riding, so the rest of the body must be relied on for stability and security instead. As well as working on remedying specific faults in the arm, achieving an improvement will also depend upon the seat, the torso and the ability to balance; see Chapter 4 The seat, Chapter 6 The upper body, and Chapter 12 Balance and coordination.

EXERCISE

25

Arm shake

This exercise helps to relax and soften wrists and arms, making it easier to carry them in a correct position.

Benefits

Whenever you feel your fingers tightening on the reins and notice tension in the wrists or arms, this is a good exercise to help relax and soften them again, allowing you to correct their position more easily. It's also very good for helping to warm up your hands on cold days!

How to do it

❏ Place the reins in one hand. With the other arm held slightly away from your side, shake the wrist back and forth, starting with slow, small movements and gradually making them brisker. Keep the fingers soft, allowing them to move with your wrist.
❏ Let the jiggling movement spread right up the whole arm to the shoulder, and becoming brisker. Imagine that someone has removed all the bones from your arm, so the movement is very free and loose.
❏ Repeat with the other arm.

DO: try to stay straight and not to lean over the arm you are shaking.

AVOID: hunching the shoulder of the arm you are shaking, as this will limit the freedom of movement. Do remember to let the chest stretch open and feel wide when you finish so the shoulder can drop back and down.

WRISTBANDS

Slip a sweatband over each wrist and you'll be surprised at how much they heighten your awareness of what your wrists are doing, particularly if you tend to over-round or hollow them. The gentle support they give will also encourage you to keep a softer wrist.

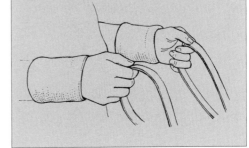

Heavy elbows

Shoulders and hands will benefit from this exercise as well as elbows and it can help improve your rein contact.

Benefits

This exercise can be helpful if you're inclined to lift your elbows outwards or to clamp them to your sides; it encourages a feeling of weight in the elbow and relaxation through the shoulders, which may also be raised and tight. It also helps you to be more aware of the position of your hands and to create a more elastic rein contact using the whole of the arm and shoulders.

How to do it

❑ Place the reins in one hand; ask someone to hold your horse if you feel this is necessary.
❑ Raise the other arm up vertically so the hand is above your head. Keep the elbow slightly flexed.
❑ Very slowly increase the flexion in the elbow, imagining as you do so that it is feeling very heavy as it sinks down towards your side. Pretend you have a brick tied to it.
❑ Once the elbow has reached your side, rotate the forearm forwards towards the horse's head so that the hand comes into the correct position to hold the reins again.

DO: keep the palm uppermost as your elbow sinks down. This helps the chest to stay feeling wide and open and the shoulders to drop down and back.

AVOID: holding your breath – you should try to breathe out slowly at the same time as your elbow is lowering.

Moving on

Try this once or twice at halt, and if your horse is steady and calm, it can then also be ridden in walk and trot.

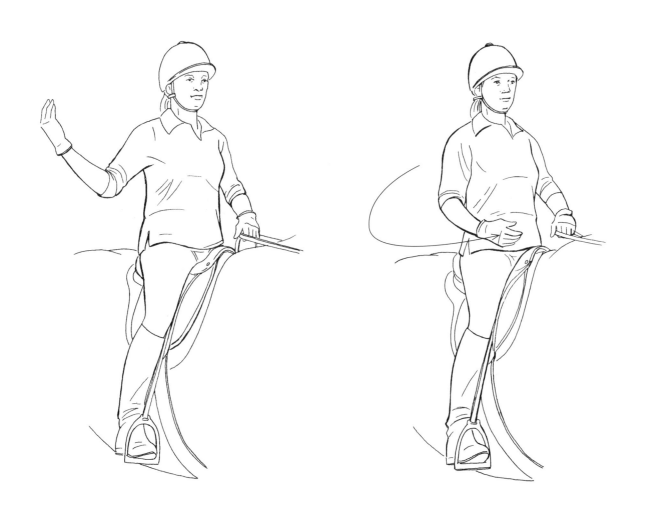

Elbow lifts and slides

This exercise will help you to relax elbows or hands that are clamped or fixed.

Benefits

This is a two phase exercise that can be done in halt or walk. It can be helpful with elbows that tend to be clamped and also if the hands tend to be fixed and low, with loss of flexion at the elbow. It can also help with 'flying' elbows, as it increases awareness of what they are doing and enables you to make a relaxed correction. It's quite subtle, so take care not to rush or exaggerate the movements.

How to do it

❏ Place the reins in one hand. Keep the other hand and arm in a normal riding position, with the upper arm perpendicular, elbow flexed and fingers curled into a soft fist as though holding the reins.
❏ Steadily and deliberately, slide the free arm forwards about 15 to 30cm (6 to 12in), keeping it parallel to the ground; you may find it helps to think of the elbow pushing the forearm.
❏ Slide the forearm back again and slightly beyond its starting point.
❏ Repeat five times, finishing so that the upper arm is once again perpendicular from the shoulder.
❏ Keeping the elbow flexed so the upper arm and forearm form a right angle, raise the forearm out to the side. Keep the forearm parallel to the ground not allowing either the hand or the elbow to lead the movement.
❏ Repeat five times and then repeat the first three steps again five more times.

DO: try to keep a feeling of weight in the elbows at all times and to keep the movements smooth, unhurried and fluid.

AVOID: lifting the elbow too high when moving it sideways away from the ribcage or it will begin to lift the shoulder; a few inches is sufficient. If you feel your shoulder beginning to rise, you've lifted your shoulder too far.

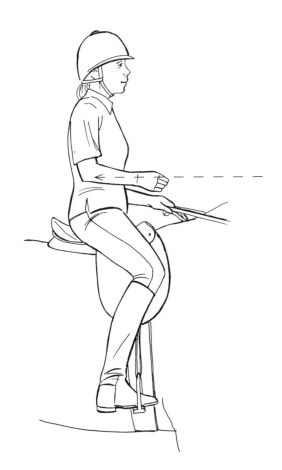

28

Soft arm

Allowing one arm to hang softly down by your side will quickly highlight any weakness in posture or lack of balance and stability in your seat.

Benefits

This exercise helps to highlight any weaknesses in balance, aid application and depth of seat. It teaches you to be less reliant on the reins for control and support, to ride forwards from the seat, legs and back, and promotes balance and confidence. Don't attempt this exercise unless your horse is steady and sensible and you are confident in your ability to control him with the reins in one hand. If in doubt, work in walk and halt with someone leading you. This exercise can also be performed on the lunge.

How to do it

❑ Place both the reins in one hand allowing the other one to hang naturally by your side. Don't hold it stiffly – there should be a slight flexion at the elbow and the fingers should be gently curved rather than pointing downwards or made into a fist. The back of your hand should be facing away from you, as this will help to keep your shoulder soft and prevent it from rounding.

❑ Ride around in walk for a few minutes. Your free arm should be sufficiently relaxed that there is a small amount of gentle swing and slight up/down movement as your horse moves beneath you.

❑ Try riding some transitions between walk and halt. Your arm should remain without stiffness in the same position, with your hand just behind your thigh. Any exaggerated movements forwards or outwards, or if you find yourself holding it rigid and motionless, stiffening the fingers or clenching the hand into a fist, will indicate that your arm is trying to compensate for tipping forwards, collapsing through the ribcage, or for loss of balance and stability in the seat. Normally this excess movement would be transferred to the rein contact, so once you have noted it, it can help you appreciate just how amazingly tolerant and forgiving our horses often are.

❑ Be aware of what your free arm is doing at all times and make positional corrections as necessary. Return to walk, check the position of your seat, align your shoulders above your hips, shake out the tension in your arm and shoulder and try again. The better your overall posture, the better your arm will be and vice versa. You should also notice a corresponding improvement in your horse's responses.

DO: try doing Exercise 25 Arm shake first to get rid of tension if your arm feels stiff. Allow your arm to hang from a soft, relaxed shoulder.

AVOID: trying to keep the arm still by holding it stiffly and rigidly as this is actually more likely to lead to unwanted movement. There will be a slight amount of movement in the arm if it and the shoulder are relaxed, but it will appear steady in relation to the horse.

Moving on

When you feel confident that you are making some progress in walk and halt transitions, introduce transitions into trot, and when ready, into canter.

Driving reins

This exercise will help relax stiff wrists and give you a feel for the reins being an extension of your whole arm, rather than simply being held in a mechanical fashion by the hands.

Benefits

There are several benefits to be gained from this exercise.

❏ It will help you gain greater sensitivity in the use of your reins as it will be harder to use them for support and almost impossible to pull on them.

❏ You will be encouraged to think more about riding your horse forwards into a soft contact instead of constricting him within it.

❏ This is also a good exercise if you're inclined to 'fiddle' with the contact and will help you establish a level feel through both reins.

❏ In terms of position, it will give you a more correct line along the forearm and rein if you tend to carry the hand either too low or too high. It also keeps the thumb on top and thereby discourages the hand from turning over so that the backs are uppermost.

How to do it

❏ Instead of holding the reins in the conventional way, hold them so they pass between thumb and forefinger first, emerging through the bottom of the hand beneath the little finger.

❏ Try walking and halting, and some turns and circles. You may find that it feels a little awkward at first, but as you begin to get used to it, you'll find a more yielding response from the horse in answer to the new softness that he feels in the rein contact.

AVOID: trying this exercise unless your horse is steady and sensible. If in doubt, try it in walk with someone leading you before trying it on your own.

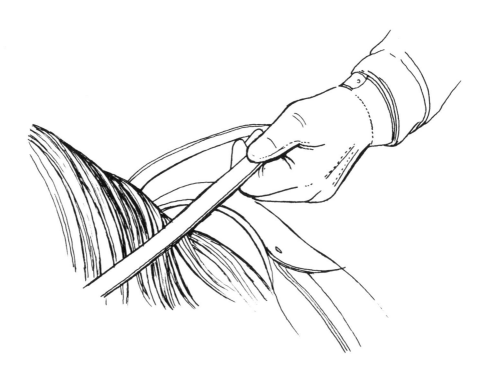

THE HANDS

'… good hands … are the result of a perfect seat and fine feeling.'

Gustav Steinbrecht 1808–1885: German riding master, teacher and author on classical horsemanship

THE EXERCISES

Supple and correctly positioned hands and wrists play an important part in achieving an effective yet sympathetic rein contact – but never forget that the whole of the arm and shoulders are involved too. As can be seen from looking at the troubleshooting section, there is a vast number of potential hand problems, but whilst addressing specific issues it's essential to remember that good hands and arms and shoulders are largely the result of a secure and independent seat and correct posture through all the rest of the body. If you become out of balance or insecure you will invariably compensate by using the rein contact for support.

TIP

If carrying a whip, the angle at which it is held can give you a clue as to what your hands (and arms) are doing. It should lie across your leg at approximately mid-thigh; if it is higher, it's usually because you are propping forwards on to your hands or are holding your hands at an incorrect angle to the wrists. And if it's sticking outwards, this is probably because the hands are turned over.

The rider's hands are too low, with fixed rigid arms, causing the whip to be held horizontally. With the whip in this position there is also a possibility that the horse may be accidentally hit on the quarters.

Finger wiggle

Try this exercise to reduce tension and stiffness should you find yourself holding the reins in an overtight grip.

Benefits

The reins should be held in lightly clenched fists. The often used comparison is to imagine that you are holding a small bird in each hand – firmly enough to keep it from escaping, but not so tightly that you throttle it. This exercise will help if you are holding the reins too tightly.

How to do it

❏ Place both reins in one hand; hold the other hand slightly to your side, fingers extended and spread apart.
❏ Give the whole of your hand a little shake, allowing the fingers to be as relaxed and floppy as possible.
❏ Allow all the fingers to relax so they begin to curl inwards. Starting with the little finger, flex each finger one at a time until all of them are closed into a soft, slightly open fist.
❏ If your arm is stiff it will affect the softness and suppleness of the fingers, so it can be a good idea to work your way up the whole arm, shaking out fingers, wrists and then the whole of the arm (see Exercise 25 Arm shake).

DO: Repeat with the other hand – even if it feels fine, it may to some extent be mirroring what the other one is doing.

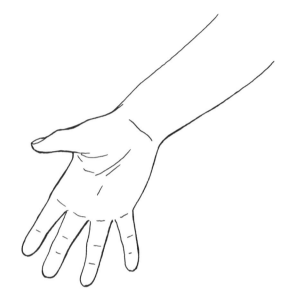

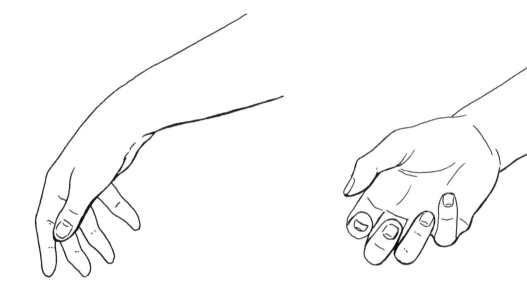

Finger touch

This exercise will help make the fingers more supple, thereby helping you to develop a better rein contact.

Benefits

Another good finger suppling exercise, which can help make your rein aids more subtle and will discourage an overtight grip on the reins. It can be done either dismounted, or one hand at a time while riding, while holding the reins with the other hand.

How to do it

❏ Touch the top of your right thumb with the pad of the index finger of the same hand, and then the second, third and small finger in turn. It is important to move the fingers towards the thumb, rather than vice versa.

❏ Repeat the exercise, this time starting with the little finger and finishing with the index finger.

❏ Repeat the first and second steps, this time with the left hand. You will probably notice a difference in flexibility and coordination between your dominant hand and the other one; this will become less apparent with practice however.

DO: make sure each finger touches the thumb – if you go too fast, you'll notice how your finger placement tends to become less accurate and you may even occasionally miss a finger out.

AVOID: looking at what you are doing. Try to get into the habit of knowing what your hands are doing without having to check.

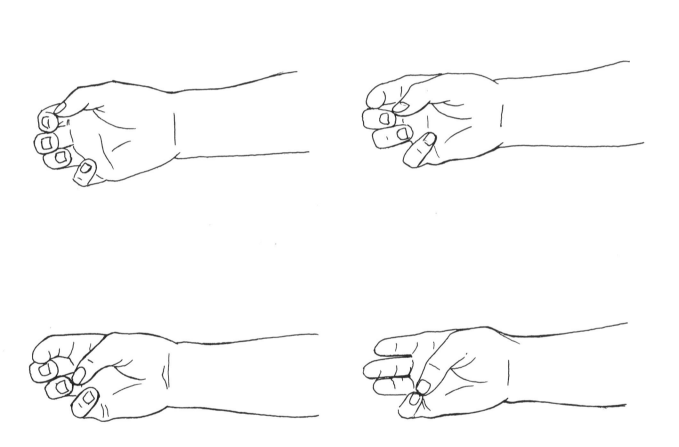

Gloves

Wearing gloves heightens your awareness of what your hands are doing and can help you correct your hand position.

Benefits

If you aren't aware of what your hands are doing it's hard to make appropriate corrections. Doing something as simple as wearing a pair of gloves increases your awareness of your hands, can help with correct thumb placement and also encourages you to be more subtle in the action of your hands on the reins.

How to do it

❏ Put on a pair of gloves – the neoprene type are good because they give a close but unconstricting fit.
❏ Preferably wear gloves that are either white or a bright colour as this makes it easier for you to use peripheral vision when necessary to check visually on your hands. It also makes it easier for someone on the ground to spot what your hands are doing, and of course if out hacking there will be the additional practical benefit in that hand signals to road users will be more visible. Adding reflective strips or dots to the backs of gloves will further increase visibility.

DO: also use gloves as a helpful tool for younger children who may still have trouble learning left and right. A different coloured glove worn on each hand – for example red on the right and blue on the left – can be used.

TIP
Improve the position of your hands while riding by imagining you are holding a mug of tea in each hand.

EXERCISE

33

Knuckle touch

This exercise helps you to keep your hands level and at the same height while stopping you from clamping your elbows.

Benefits

This is an easy way of checking on what your hands are doing, ensuring that they are at the same height and that you aren't tending to draw one backwards. If you know that you are inclined to fix the hands downwards, it's also a good exercise to practise frequently, as it encourages a better hand position and discourages clamped elbows.

How to do it

❑ Slowly bring both knuckles together so that they lightly touch.
❑ Try this not just when working on straight lines, but also through turns and circles, as it will encourage you to think about influencing the horse using the whole of your body and a supporting outside rein.

DO: keep a light contact with your knuckles; don't force them rigidly together.

AVOID: looking downwards at your hands.

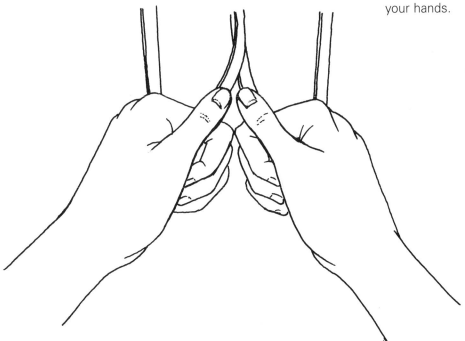

Rein length

Your reins must be the same length in order to keep your horse straight and moving forwards into a level contact with your hands.

Benefits

It's important to have both reins the same length if you are to create a straight horse moving forwards into a level contact. It's not always easy to tell and you can sometimes be deceived into thinking they are the same when this isn't the case. This exercise provides you with a way of quickly checking.

TIP

Make sure the reins are a comfortable width for you to hold. If they are too narrow or too wide it can make it difficult for you to hold them correctly.

How to do it

❏ Use reins with grips stitched on, and simply check that you are holding both the reins the same number of grips away from the bit. Rein grips will also help prevent the reins from slipping away through one or both hands, or becoming uneven or too long.

❏ If you don't have, or don't want to use, reins with grips, slide a coloured elastic band on to each, wrapped tightly round several times so they are a tight fit and won't move, and check that they both lie the same distance from the bit along each rein. Coloured bands are more easily visible, so that only a quick glance is needed to check. Use them as a reference point, holding each rein at the same distance from each band. Alternatively, use a piece of coloured electrical insulation tape.

DO: check each time before you ride that the elastic bands on the reins haven't become displaced.

Bridged reins

This exercise helps you learn to maintain a correct and consistent length of rein.

Benefits

Riders are more likely to be guilty of having reins too long than too short and this can lead to the hands becoming unlevel, held too far apart, or drawn backwards in order to maintain the contact, as well as consequent postural problems such as getting behind the movement. In addition to reduced rider control, the contact is often intermittent, jerky and irritating to the horse, possibly causing injury and very likely to lead to bit evasions. Even though you start with the reins at a correct length, they sometimes gradually slip through your fingers and become too long without your being aware of it. This exercise helps you to rectify bad habits and learn to maintain a more correct and consistent length of rein.

How to do it

❏ Bridge the reins as shown in the picture below. Check that they are the same length, as well as being short enough.

❏ Younger children and more novice riders may find it easier to tie their reins in a knot instead, holding them just in front of the knot. In both instances it will also discourage the hands from being held too wide apart, as well as riding on too long a rein.

❏ To a certain extent it will also limit any tendency to draw one hand upwards, downwards or backwards, but more importantly still, it will increase your awareness of this happening so you can make a conscious correction.

DO: practise riding in walk and asking for transitions to halt before trying other gaits, turns and circles.

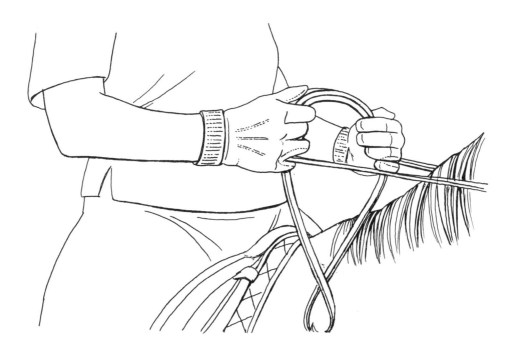

Neck touch

This exercise will help you develop a steady contact on the reins. You can also use it to check that you aren't using the reins to help you balance.

Benefits

This is a good way of increasing your awareness of what your hands are doing and of helping you learn to develop a contact which is steady, but not fixed and rigid. It also encourages you to carry your hand towards the horse's mouth a little and helps you to think about riding the horse forwards into the contact.

TIP

When working in rising trot, think of your hips moving towards your hands, so you reduce the likelihood of using the reins for support.

How to do it

❏ Keeping the reins in both hands, stick out the little finger of each and rest them lightly against the horse's neck on either side.

❏ Try to maintain a light but constant contact with the tips of the fingers without forcibly digging them into the neck muscle to keep them there. If you keep losing contact, it's often an indication of stiffness in the shoulders and arms, but it can also be a symptom of stiffness elsewhere.

❏ This is also a good exercise for checking that you aren't using the rein contact to help you balance, especially in rising trot, or that you aren't pushing, pulling or lifting with your hands when applying leg aids.

DO: shorten your reins if necessary.

AVOID: straightening and stiffening your little fingers – when you stick them out, keep them slightly curved and maintain the flexion in your elbows.

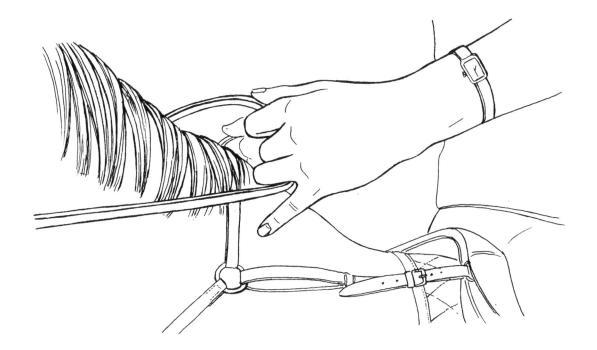

THE LEGS

'Noisy legs will confuse the horse ... the horse sometimes interprets the rider's movements as aids when they are not intended to be, and at other times will ignore them, although they are intended as aids.'

Adolph Kaestner: 19th century German author on classical horsemanship

THE EXERCISES

37. Sitting to the trot with stirrups

38. Side leg lift

39. Knee circles

40. Leg swing

41. Knee push

42. Ankle grab

The rider's legs should hang in a close contact with the horse's sides, but without gripping or clinging. This requires flexibility in the hip joints and muscles around the lower back and pelvic region as well as in the thighs. Any tension or tightness in the upper leg or gripping with the knee will prevent the lower leg from making contact properly, as well as restricting the ability to stretch the legs down. If these muscles are tight, attempting to push the legs down further with the ankle beneath the hips will cause the upper body to tilt forwards and the rider to perch on the fork of his seat. Trying to sit up straight again will cause either extreme hollowing of the back, or the thighs and knees to rise back up again.

As well as relaxed and supple muscles, it's important to have good mobility in the joints because the hip, knee and ankle joints act as shock absorbers, and they must be softly flexed in order to work effectively.

On the girth

Using or putting your leg 'on the girth' is a term commonly used, but in practice this is not always possible or even desirable – whether you can do so depends on several factors, such as your horse's conformation, your shape, your level of riding, the type of saddle and even the positioning of the stirrup bars on the saddle. It is best, therefore, not to take the phrase too literally.

Choosing an appropriate stirrup length

The length of your stirrups depends on the work you want to do – generally longer for flatwork and shorter for jumping. Riding with a longer stirrup length allows you to have more of your leg in contact with your horse's sides, to sit more deeply into the saddle and to give more subtle and precise aids. A shorter stirrup length enables you to take your weight out of the saddle and stay in balance with the movement of your horse over fences, and when galloping. When hacking, choose a length between the two extremes, allowing a secure position that can be adapted according to terrain, and which doesn't impede the effective use of your leg aids.

It may be desirable to achieve a 'longer' leg position for flatwork but you can only lengthen your stirrups as much as your depth of seat allows, the exaggeratedly long, almost straight-legged 'clothes-peg' posture adopted by many modern dressage riders is not necessarily the ideal. A true classical seat, as shown by the Spanish Riding School, shows a pronounced angle in the hips and knees, allowing the rider to sit deeply and securely and enables the joints to work as shock absorbers.

Stirrup problems

Your stirrups may be too long if:
- ❏ you keep losing your stirrup irons
- ❏ the irons keep sliding up your instep and your toes point downwards
- ❏ you feel you are constantly having to reach for your stirrups with your toes, instead of keeping your heels slightly lower than your toes comfortably
- ❏ you need to use the reins to help you balance, especially in rising trot
- ❏ you lack control over your legs, which swing around on your horse's sides and flap ineffectively when giving leg aids
- ❏ you perch on the front of your seat instead of sitting on your seat bones, tend to tip forwards with your upper body and hollow your lower back
- ❏ you tend to get left behind when jumping, or stand up in the stirrups and get too far forwards.

Your stirrups may be too short if:
- ❏ your seat is pushed to the back of the saddle, instead of being in the central, deepest part of it
- ❏ you rise exaggeratedly high in rising trot and find it hard to sit to the trot and canter
- ❏ your knees stick out over the front of the saddle
- ❏ you have difficulty in using your legs, as they feel locked into position.

TIP

You can judge whether the stirrups are the right length before mounting. Slide the stirrup irons down the leathers, put the knuckle of one hand on the stirrup bar and draw the leather along your under-arm. When the length is roughly right for hacking, the bottom of the iron should just reach into your armpit.

Sitting to the trot with stirrups

Correct posture is essential if you are to master sitting to the trot successfully, in addition to keeping hip, knee and ankle joints softly flexed and acting as shock absorbers.

Benefits

Many riders find it easier to sit to the trot without stirrups than with them because without stirrups they can't push against them. Only the smallest amount of bracing against the stirrups can lead to bouncing in the saddle, so it's important that the knee and ankle as well as the hip joint remain softly flexed.

How to do it

❏ Go forwards to sitting trot from walk, rather than rising trot, as your joints and muscles will be more relaxed. Breathe out as your horse moves into the trot and keep the upper body upright and elegant as the seat and lower back will be better able to absorb the movement.

❏ Imagine that you are just about to kneel down, as this will help you to keep the legs stretching down, drawing the seat more deeply into the saddle, while at the same time keeping the knees soft. This reduces the risk of the heels being pushed down over strongly, causing the seat to be boosted up away from the saddle. It will also help to keep the lower leg lightly in contact with the horse's sides.

❏ Do only as many strides of sitting to the trot as are comfortable for you and your horse. The moment either of you begins to struggle, return to walk or go into a rising trot. Start with a slow jog trot, increasing the activity as you feel able to cope with it. Place the reins in one hand if necessary, and hold the front of the saddle with the other to help balance and stabilize yourself.

❏ As you find yourself able to sit easily and well for longer periods, try going from rising to sitting to the trot and back to rising again. Your horse's speed, rhythm, length of stride, balance and outline should not change.

DO: remember to allow the horse to lift and carry your seat along, rather than you forcing it down into the saddle. See also Exercise 12 Riding without stirrups.

AVOID: feeling that you have to sit to the trot when moving from canter to trot. Unless you are very well balanced and supple, it's easier to rise to the trot after canter rather than bouncing or gripping yourself down into the saddle. It will also make it easier for you to quickly establish the rhythm and speed with less advanced horses, which will most likely lack the musculature and the strength to cope with the rider sitting deeply during the transition.

EXERCISE 38

Side leg lift

This exercise will help you to develop a deeper seat and 'longer' leg.

Benefits

This exercise stretches the muscles at the top of the thigh, helping to stretch open and deepen the seat while enabling the leg to stretch down. You may find it easier to move one leg more than the other, but try to move them by the same amount so you do not further increase the dominance of the 'better' one. Ask someone to hold your horse if you cannot control it safely with the reins held in one hand.

How to do it

❏ With your horse at halt, place both the reins in your left hand and the right one on the front of the saddle for balance and support.

❏ Remove your right foot from the stirrup and, keeping the knee flexed, move the right leg outwards away from the saddle. Move the entire leg so that the thigh just comes out of contact. Hold for a count of three to five according to how difficult you find it, then relax and slowly allow the leg to come back into contact with the saddle again.

❏ Change the reins into your right hand, place the left one on the front of the saddle and repeat with the left leg.

❏ If the thigh muscles begin to cramp, it may be because you are trying to move the leg out further than you are ready for. Bring the affected leg up and forwards over the front of the saddle flap to relieve the discomfort.

DO: keep the upper body vertical. Take care not to lean forwards or backwards, curl up through your ribcage, lean to one side or hunch your shoulders.

AVOID: letting the leg fall back abruptly on to the horse's sides.

Knee circles

This exercise will help you to develop independent use of the legs, to sit deeper and relax the upper leg muscles.

Benefits

This exercise helps relax the muscles of the upper thigh and round the hip joint and teaches independent action of both legs. It also helps you to sit deeper. Ask someone to hold your horse if you feel you cannot control it safely with the reins held in one hand.

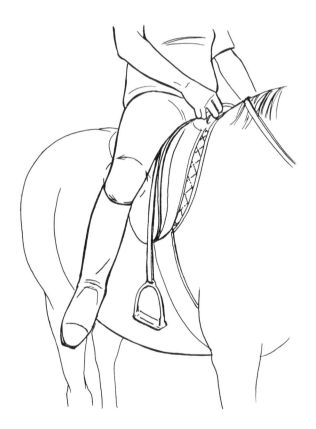

How to do it

- ❏ With your horse in halt, place both reins in the left hand and take your right foot out of the stirrup. Place your right hand on the front of the saddle in order to support yourself.
- ❏ Lift your right leg up a little by increasing the flexion in your knee and position it slightly away from the saddle. Draw a circle in the air with your knee about the same diameter as a tennis ball. Circle it ten times in both clockwise and anti-clockwise directions.
- ❏ Repeat with the left leg.

DO: keep the toe of your foot in line with the knee – don't allow it to twist at an angle to the shin.

AVOID: leaning forwards or backwards – try to keep your upper body vertical.

TIP
Your feet should be positioned directly beneath your seat so that if you were to be lifted off the horse and then set on the ground in the same position, you would remain in balance and wouldn't topple over.

40

Leg swing

This exercise will help improve coordination and independent use of the legs.

Benefits

This exercise helps stretch the front of the thigh muscles and 'lengthen' the legs. It also helps improve coordination and the independent action of both legs. Ask someone to hold your horse if you feel you cannot control it safely with the reins held in one hand.

How to do it

❏ With your horse at halt, place both the reins in your left hand; hold the front of the saddle with the right hand to help you stay balanced.

❏ Take your right foot out of the saddle and swing it first slightly forwards and then slightly backwards. Keep the toe pointing forwards, move the leg from the hip and keep the knee slightly flexed. Check that your upper body remains vertical and that you do not tip forwards on to the fork of your seat.

❏ Repeat five times, then switch the reins to the other hand and repeat with the other leg.

DO: take care not to kick your horse accidentally – keep your movements smooth and controlled rather than abrupt and jerky.

AVOID: swinging the leg so much that it rocks your seat up and out of contact with the saddle.

Knee push

If you tend to grip with your knees, or your knees creep upwards as you ride, this exercise will help you drop your weight down through the leg.

Benefits

If you find that your knees tend to creep upwards, which can often happen when riding turns and circles, this exercise can help. Even if the knees don't creep up, it can be a good way of encouraging the weight to drop down through the front of the thigh, helping to stretch the leg down and sit deeper. It also helps to discourage gripping with the knees. Ask someone to hold or lead your horse if you feel you cannot control it safely with the reins held in one hand.

How to do it

❑ Place both the reins into one hand and place the index finger of the other hand on the thigh just above the knee. Gently but firmly press down with it, relaxing the upper thigh as much as possible at the same time.
❑ Repeat with the other hand and leg.

DO: check your straightness after doing this exercise as it can encourage you to collapse through the side of your waist after doing it.

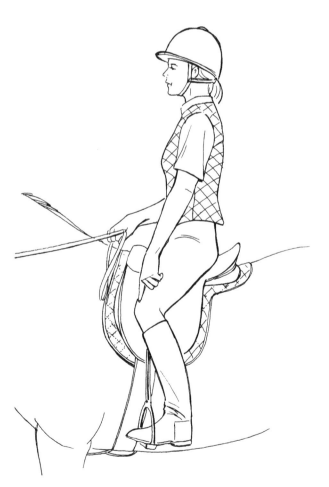

DEVELOP A 'LONGER' LEG WITH CAUTION!

When trying to develop a 'longer' leg, don't try for too much too quickly; it's a classic mistake made by pupils (and just as often their instructors), but you should never weaken the seat in your enthusiasm to let the stirrups down. Bear in mind also that what may feel fine in walk may not be quite so easy to maintain when you begin to trot and canter. Be ready to return to your previous stirrup length if you find that, after all, you aren't quite ready for it, rather than struggle on.

EXERCISE

42

Ankle grab

This is another exercise that will help you encourage the leg to stretch down through the thigh, improving the leg contact.

Benefits

This exercise helps stretch the muscles at the front of the thigh, making it easier for you to stretch your leg down and keep it in a close contact with the horse's sides. Ask someone to hold your horse if you cannot control it safely with the reins held in one hand.

How to do it

❏ With your horse in halt, place the reins in your left hand. Remove your right foot from the stirrup.

❏ Bend your right knee, bringing the foot up towards your seat. Take hold of the ankle joint with your right hand and press gently downwards into the front of the thigh, without tipping your body.

❏ Hold for a count of five and then release. Change your reins over into your right hand and repeat with the left leg.

DO: keep your upper body vertical – don't lean backwards or forwards or raise your seat from the saddle.

AVOID: leaning to the side while trying this exercise.

THE FEET AND ANKLES

'… he must be able to apply his aids so well that nobody sees which hand or leg is addressing the horse.'

Gaspard de Saunier 1663–1748: French soldier, equestrian and author on classical horsemanship

THE EXERCISES

43. Ankle circling

44. Toe straightener

45. Heel deepener

Getting the position of your feet right is often neglected, but if it is incorrect this will affect the subtlety and effectiveness of the leg aids and can drastically affect balance, suppleness and security throughout the rest of the body. The feet should be allowed to hang parallel to the horse's sides, with the ball of each foot placed squarely across the tread of the stirrup irons. It's not a good idea to twist the stirrup leathers round the irons to shorten them because quite apart from being difficult to get them both level, it causes the irons to hang at an incorrect angle.

Important facts about stirrup irons

- Fitting irons with rubber treads will help to stop the feet sliding around in them. It is also a good idea to lightly sandpaper the soles of new leather boots, or boots that have just been resoled, to minimize the risk of slipping.
- Irons should be a matching pair. Heavier, German-type irons will swing about less if your feet accidentally slip out of them, which makes them easier to regain.
- The stirrup leather should be the same width as the slot in the iron through which it is threaded. If too narrow a leather is used, the iron is likely to hang at an angle.
- Stirrup irons should allow a 6mm (¼in) clearance on either side of the foot; less may lead to a foot becoming wedged, whilst more could allow it to slip through.
- For the sake of safety as well as position, always wear sensible and appropriate footwear – flat-soled, with a small, defined heel of not less than 13mm (½in) or more than 25mm (1in).
- Turn the iron towards you so that the leather lies flat against your leg. If the edge digs into you, the discomfort will affect position and can cause bruising.
- Angled irons are not a good idea as they can force muscles to stretch too rapidly and can lead to fatigue, discomfort, cramp and even injury. They can also end up ultimately distorting the position and locking the lower leg.

- Similarly, tying the stirrup irons to the girth to try to stabilize the lower leg position is neither safe nor sensible, especially if a foot is trapped in a fall. In both the short and the long term, it's better to learn how to control your body properly, than to rely on a quick fix.

LOSING A STIRRUP IRON

Losing a stirrup can put you off balance, affecting your security and control, which causes a degree of panic in some. If you practise kicking a foot free of the iron and regaining it, this will help boost your confidence so you can cope in the event of this happening. Try to place your foot back in the iron without looking down, first of all while in halt, then in walk, and as you grow more adept and confident, in trot and canter. Turning your toe inwards and bringing it up slightly as you search for the iron with your foot will help. Use the opposite stirrup for increased support and see if you can still maintain the flow and rhythm of the gait in which you are working. Practise with each foot so you become equally proficient with both.

Ankle circling

You can do this exercise to make the ankle joint more supple wherever you are, at home, at work or when in the saddle.

Benefits

This exercise helps to increase suppleness in stiff ankle joints. It's also one that can be done at home, or at work, or any time when you're sitting down.

How to do it

❏ Take one foot out of the stirrup and circle it in a clockwise direction. Imagining drawing a circle in the air with your toe will give you a more complete range of movement through the ankle joint.
❏ Next, circle it in the same way in an anti-clockwise direction.
❏ Repeat with the other foot.

DO: make small circles with the toes to begin with, gradually increasing their size as the ankle joint becomes more flexible.

AVOID: doing more circles in one direction, or with one foot, than the other – try to keep track of them.

TIP
Tension in the neck can also lead to stiffness in the ankles, so doing some exercises for this part of your body can also help (see Chapter 5, The head and neck).

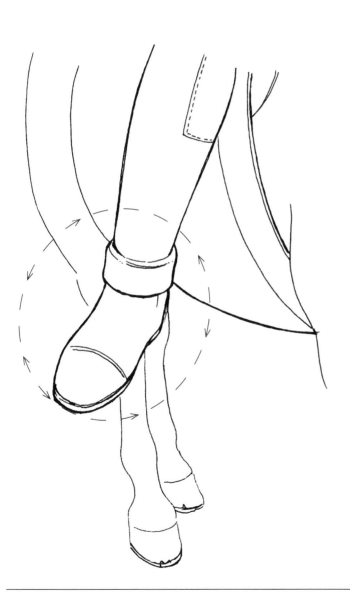

EXERCISE

44

Toe straightener

This exercise can help you to sit deep in the saddle as well as correct a faulty toe position.

Benefits

Where toes tend to stick outwards, the correction needs to be made from the hip and through the whole of the leg. In addition to helping bring the feet into a more parallel position with the horse's sides, this exercise also helps to stretch open and deepen the seat. You may also find it helpful to try Exercise 04, Heel turn.

How to do it

❏ In halt, place the reins in one hand, and use two fingers of the other hand to hold the front arch of the saddle for support and balance.
❏ Raise the right seatbone a little, move it across as far away from the left one as possible and then settle it down again on the saddle.
❏ Raise the left seatbone, move it across as far away from the right seatbone as possible and then settle it down again on the saddle.

DO: check on straightness after doing the exercise – it can be easy to shift one seatbone across further than the other.

TIP

After riding, check the inside of your boots to see where the grease from your horse's coat has accumulated. If you've been turning your toes outwards, or gripping up with your heels, you'll see that most of the grease is at the back of the boot instead of to the inside.

Heel deepener

This exercise can help you overcome stiffness in the ankle joint and to stretch tight calf muscles, helping you to achieve a more correct and stable leg position.

Benefits

If you have difficulty lowering your heels, it may be due to tight calf muscles as well as to stiff ankle joints. Try using this exercise in conjunction with Exercise 43, Ankle circling, to remedy the problem.

How to do it

❏ In halt, take hold of a handful of mane or the neckstrap, together with the reins, to help keep your balance, so you don't accidentally pull backwards on the horse's mouth or bump down in the saddle.
❏ Make sure that the balls of your feet are correctly positioned across the treads of the stirrups.
❏ Stand up on your toes in the stirrups; hold for a count of five.
❏ Slowly allow the ankle joints to relax, letting the heels drop downwards. At the same time, gradually flex the knees and allow your seat to sink gently down into the saddle.

AVOID: over-correcting this problem, as an excessively deep heel is just as undesirable and creates its own difficulties. Ideally the heel should be level with, or very slightly lower than, the toes.

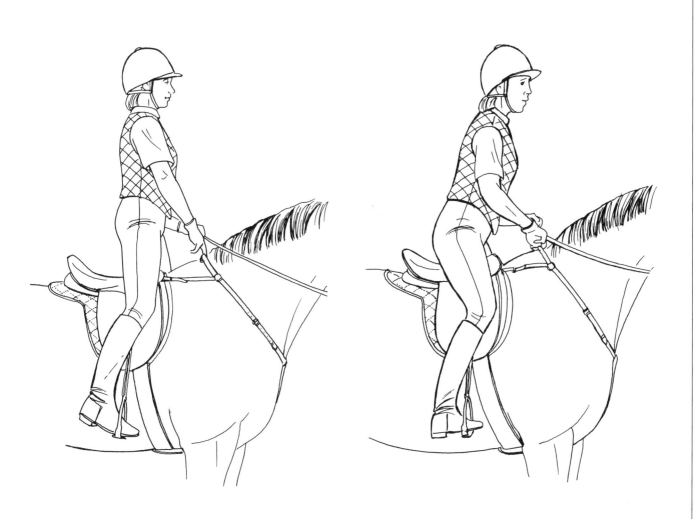

12 BALANCE AND COORDINATION

'The rider who has no balance himself cannot give his horse balance.'

Ludwig Hunersdorf 1748–1813: German riding master, author on classical horsemanship

THE EXERCISES

Balance and coordination go hand in hand with each other; poor balance will lead to poor coordination, and vice versa. Lack of balance will also cause both you and your horse to tire more quickly as a result of having to use increased muscular effort to compensate. It can also sap your horse's confidence as he struggles to maintain his own equilibrium, and as a result it can make him more liable to injuries. Balance is important for your own safety too, since, more than strength, it enables you to remain in the saddle if your horse does something unexpected.

Coordination is an equally important attribute, the rider needing to synchronize the movements of about 200 bones and over 500 muscles in order to remain in harmony with, and to direct, the horse. Poor coordination will affect all of your work, from the most basic to the most advanced of movements, directly influencing your position and the application and timing of your aids.

Whether you are struggling with balance and coordination, find it hard to 'multi-task', or simply wish to fine tune your abilities, there are a number of exercises that can help.

Children

Children may have an enviable degree of suppleness, but as they grow up, periods of rapid growth and changes in shape can sometimes create problems with balance and coordination that adults don't have to contend with. Up to the age of puberty, children increase in height by an average of around 6cm (2½in) a year – and not at a steady rate, but in spurts, with a major growth spurt occurring between 8–13 years in girls and 10–15 years in boys. This can sometimes result in a degree of clumsiness and lack of coordination, while changes in body shape at puberty can also lead to self-consciousness, affecting riding posture.

TIP

If you don't have too over-developed a sense of dignity and fancy trying something a little different, then vaulting can also be a good way of helping improve your balance, coordination, confidence, strength, flexibility and sense of rhythm. It can be as much fun for adults as children, and in the UK a number of 'have-a-go' events are held around the country each year. However, if such events are not held near you it can be well worth thinking about joining a club that participates in this discipline.

Rising to the trot

Requiring both balance and coordination, when performed correctly rising to the trot should be relatively effortless.

Benefits

Rising to the trot is something with which novice riders often struggle initially but, surprisingly, it is often done quite poorly by more experienced riders as well. It is very much an exercise in both balance and coordination. Correctly performed it should be possible to move from sitting to the trot to rising to it with ease, with no feeling of putting in any extra exertion, and the movement itself should be relatively effortless. On the lunge, rising to the trot can also be practised without reins as a way of checking that the rider isn't relying on them to even the smallest degree to support himself during the rising phase.

How to do it

❏ Ask your horse to move into an active, forward-going trot, as this will make it easier for you to work on your rising.
❏ Don't try to push against or stand up in your stirrups as this will cause you to rise too high and your lower legs are likely to swing around. Keep your knees soft and flexed, imagining that you are just about to kneel down, and this will help prevent you from pushing against your stirrups. It will also make it easier for you to maintain your lower leg in contact with your horse's sides and to remain supple through the hips.
❏ Allowing your upper body to incline forwards very slightly from the hips, let your horse's back generate the push that moves your seat upwards. Avoid exaggerating the height you rise to, as this can result in tight, raised shoulders, stiffness in the lower back, increased likelihood of twisting as you rise, loss of lower leg contact,

loss of balance, general jerkiness in your movements and less control over the 'down' phase of the rising trot.
❏ Only rise as high as the momentum of the horse's back pushes you. With some this may mean that your seat barely moves out of the saddle and your rising becomes almost imperceptible. This is absolutely fine, because the closer your seat remains to the saddle, the greater your security and the more in harmony with your horse's trot you are likely to be.
❏ Your hips should move in a forward as well as an upward direction. Thinking of your navel travelling forwards towards your hands may help, and may also reduce any tendency for the hands to be used for support.

Establish an active, forward-going trot.

❏ Although gravity will take care of the 'down' phase of the rising trot, make sure you keep in full control of the movement so you land softly in the saddle and there is no accompanying sensation of the horse's back dipping beneath you, or change in his head carriage. At the same time the legs remain in close contact with the horse's sides. Should you need to use them, this sitting phase of rising to the trot is the best moment to do so.

DO: also try the exercises 48 Hovering trot, 47 Meeting the wind and 51 Rising to the trot without stirrups, all in this chapter, to help improve and refine your work in rising to the trot.

AVOID: raising your shoulders – allow the horse's back to push you from beneath, rather than trying to haul yourself forcibly up out of the saddle.

TIP

The sitting phase of rising to the trot is the best time to close your legs and ask for more impulsion.

Allow the horse's back to generate the push that moves your seat upwards and begins the rising.

Meeting the wind

This is a Connected Riding exercise that will improve the balance of your upper body

Benefits

Few people walk in balance at the best of times, and when riding this shortcoming becomes greatly magnified. This Connected Riding exercise helps address this – it is beneficial for those who tend to get behind the movement and will generally improve the smoothness and fluidity of rising to the trot. It is also good for anyone who tends to lean back and stiffen through downward transitions. It improves balance and also helps open up the shoulders. Although it may feel as though you are leaning or tipping forwards at first, it's more a matter of coming forwards into a harmonious balance with your horse. It's very subtle but extremely effective, and one of those exercises which really does need to be tried to appreciate the benefits fully. You'll need

assistance from someone else while on the ground – take it in turns to work with a friend and to help each other.

How to do it

❏ Imagine you are walking head on into a gentle wind – not the sort you want to put your head down and battle against, but one you can gently lean into and which slightly supports you. Your partner helps by placing a hand on your upper chest to mimic the effect of the wind, not pushing or holding you up, but just providing a very light and gentle resistance.

❏ Keep your knees relaxed and slightly flexed, carry your weight over the ball of your feet and look ahead – don't be tempted to look down to see what's happening. Avoid bending forwards from the hips in an exaggerated manner, as this will affect the natural 'S' shape of your spine and will load your lower back.

❏ When you achieve the correct balance it will literally feel as though you are lightly and easily floating forwards across the ground, taking longer and more effortless steps. Once you have this feeling on two feet, try to replicate it when in the saddle. You may find it will help at first if you place the reins in one hand (if safe to do so) and place the other on your upper chest, as when your partner was assisting you.

❏ It can be especially helpful when asking for downward transitions and halts, when many riders ask too forcefully, and frequently fall out of balance. With the rider sitting more softly and in better balance, the horse will find it easier to engage his quarters and move smoothly forwards into these changes of gait with increased accuracy and minimal resistance.

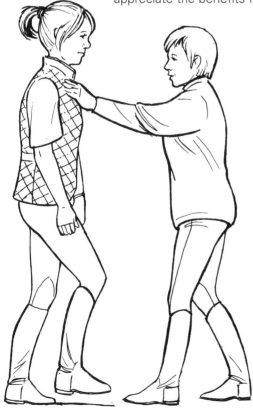

48

Hovering trot

Practising riding in this position will help improve your balance, your flexibility in hip, knee and ankle joints and the stability in your lower leg.

Benefits

Practising trotting in this position is helpful in improving your balance. It also encourages you to allow knee, hip and ankle joints to flex and work efficiently as shock absorbers, and it develops stability in the lower leg. It's also an excellent way of preparing for learning to jump if you are a novice, and is a position that riders often adopt when going across country in canter or gallop.

How to do it

❏ Shorten your stirrups between one and three holes from your usual flatwork length, depending on how long you normally ride.

❏ Ask the horse for an active, regular and forward-going trot. Once this is established, adopt a hovering position, where your seat is raised slightly out of the saddle and you are neither sitting nor rising. Incline your upper body slightly forwards and slide your seat back a little at the same time so that it acts as a counterbalance. Keep the knee and ankle joints flexed and allow your heels to drop so they are slightly lower than the toes. Check that the balls of the feet are placed squarely across the stirrup treads.

❏ Should you lean forwards too far, or allow the lower leg to slip forwards or backwards instead of remaining beneath you, you'll lose your balance and fall back into the saddle. Similarly if you stiffen through the knee, hip or ankle joints instead of absorbing the movement of the horse through them, you'll also begin to lose your balance and will find yourself trying to use grip to compensate, which you may find will tire you quickly.

❏ When you get it just right you'll find this position easy to maintain for extended periods without the need to use the horse's neck for support. Hold a handful of mane initially until you can consistently maintain your balance so as to avoid leaning on, or accidentally jerking on, the rein contact. Once you reach this point, try the exercise in canter, too.

DO: keep your back flat.

AVOID: looking down, as this will make it hard to keep your balance.

Round the world

This exercise will improve the rider's balance, agility and coordination and can help to build confidence in children.

Benefits

This can be a good exercise for increasing balance, agility and coordination, and also for promoting confidence. However, it's one that is more appropriate for children, rather than teenagers and adults. Ponies generally tend to be more tolerant of such gymnastics, although this should never be taken for granted. Their smaller size makes it easier for a teacher or helper to assist, and the lighter weight and greater degree of suppleness in children make it easier for them to succeed without causing discomfort to the pony.

SAFETY FIRST!

Safety is very important, because at various points during this exercise the rider is potentially in a very vulnerable position. Always ensure the pony used is steady and quiet and is being held by a dismounted helper. Avoid encouraging the child to rush through the exercise, because this is more likely to lead to loss of balance and coordination than to improve it, and increases the chances of the pony accidentally getting kicked by the rider's legs. Allow the child to hold on to the saddle for support if they wish and offer extra support if necessary.

How to do it

❏ While an assistant holds the pony, the rider takes his feet out of the stirrups, which he crosses over the pony's neck, knots the reins and lets go of them.
❏ Going anti-clockwise, the rider swings his right leg over the pony's neck in front of him, so he is sitting sideways on the saddle on the pony's near side.
❏ The rider then swings the left leg round and over the pony's hindquarters, so he ends up sitting facing backwards.
❏ Next the rider swings his right leg over the pony's quarters, so he is now sitting sideways again, but this time facing out from the pony's off side.
❏ Finally, the rider swings the left leg over the pony's neck again so that he is once again facing forwards, having completed a 360-degree turn in the saddle.
❏ Repeat it once again, this time going in the opposite (clockwise) direction. Most riders will find it easier going in one direction than the other initially, so this exercise will also help to discourage one-sided preferences.

DO: take care that the pony doesn't get kicked in the head, quarters or sides by the rider's feet as they swing round.

AVOID: making very timid or nervous children do this exercise.

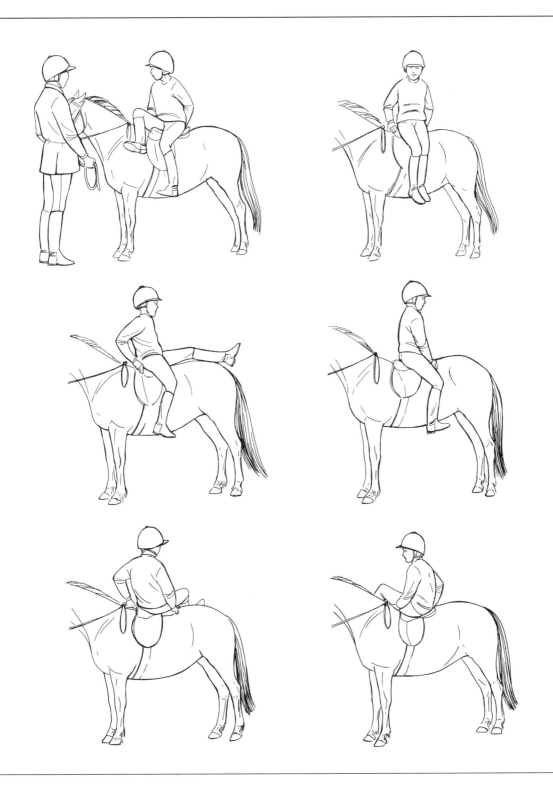

Half scissors

This is another exercise for children that will help improve balance, coordination, confidence and agility.

Benefits

The same comments and safety provisos as for Exercise 49 Round the world apply to this exercise, which also aims to help children improve balance, coordination, confidence and agility.

How to do it

❑ While an assistant holds the pony, the rider takes his feet out of the stirrups, crosses them over the pony's neck, knots the reins and lets go of them.

❑ Going anti-clockwise, the rider swings his right leg over the pony's neck in front of him, so he is sitting in a side-saddle position.

❑ The rider then brings his left hand in front of him so that he holds the front of the saddle. He then moves his right hand behind his body to hold the back of the saddle.

❑ Supporting his weight on his hands, the rider then swivels his body round so that he is leaning forwards over the pony's back.

❑ He then swings his right leg over the back of the saddle, transferring his right hand from the back to the front of the saddle as he does so, ending up astride and facing forwards once more. This step often ends up being a bit of a scramble at first, but with practice and as strength, agility, balance and coordination improve, it can be completed in a continuous fluid sequence of movement. Repeat in the opposite direction.

DO: take care that the pony doesn't get kicked in the head or quarters by the rider's feet as they swing round.

AVOID: making nervous or very timid children do this exercise.

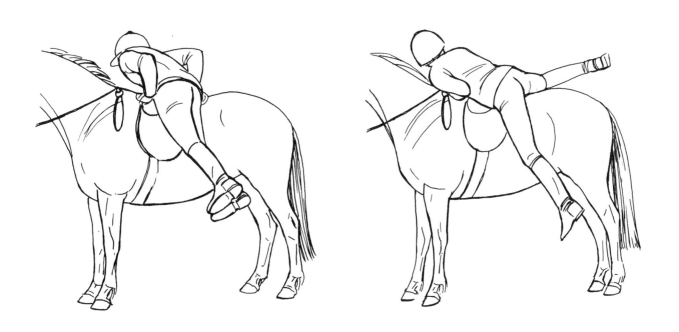

Rising to the trot without stirrups

This exercise can improve your technique in rising to the trot though only when it is done in moderation.

Benefits

This can be a helpful way of improving your rising to the trot if you are inclined to push against your stirrups or rise too high; however, it can be tiring so should only be performed for short periods.

TIP

This is not an exercise that suits everyone. If, having tried it, you find it makes you feel as though you are over-accentuating the forward/upward movement of the hips, raising your shoulders or becoming stiffer through your back, then stop.

How to do it

❏ Take your feet out of the stirrups, which you then cross so your feet don't get tangled in them and they don't bounce irritatingly against your horse's sides.

❏ Establish an active sitting trot. Raise your toes slightly, keeping your knees flexed and close to the saddle but without gripping, and allow the upward push of the horse's back to initiate each upward and forward rising movement of your hips. Take care that you don't lock through your hips as you reach the highest point of your rising.

❏ After a few strides, return to sitting to the trot, taking care not to slump as you do so; check that you are still breathing regularly and not holding your breath. When you are ready, try a few more strides of rising trot, alternating it with further periods of sitting to the trot or rest in walk.

DO: use a handful of mane or the neckstrap to help you keep your balance if necessary, but don't use it to pull yourself up out of the saddle.

AVOID: raising your shoulders to try and help you rise; let the movement come from the hips. Furthermore, avoid doing the exercise to excess because this is likely to lead to you gripping with your knees, and also stiffening through your lower back.

Rein release

This exercise will show if you are relying too much on the reins to balance yourself or to steer and it will help you learn to rely more on the use of your legs to keep the horse straight.

Benefits

By giving and then retaking your reins for a few strides, you can check that you are not relying on them for balance. Supporting yourself on the reins not only reduces the subtlety of your rein aids, but also your sensitivity to feedback from the horse via the reins. It can also create discomfort, causing him to resist through his head, neck and mouth. This exercise will also make you more aware of any tendency to be over-reliant on rein contact for steering and will encourage you to make more use of your legs to keep your horse straight.

How to do it

❏ Establish a good balance and regular rhythm in walk. Allow the hands to go forwards just sufficiently to ease the tension on the reins and allow them to become slightly slack.

❏ Avoid thrusting your hands forwards abruptly and without warning. Ease them forwards smoothly and gradually so it doesn't take your horse by surprise and cause him to lose his own concentration and balance.

❏ After riding forwards on a slack rein for a few strides, carefully and gradually retake the contact again.

❏ Having practised in walk, try the same exercise both sitting and rising to the trot. If your hands and arms tend to move around when the contact is slackened and you are no longer able to use it for support, it's an indicator that you are not entirely in balance.

DO: check your basic alignment (see Chapter 1 The basics) if you find that your balance is adversely affected when you surrender the reins.

AVOID: stiffening your arms in an attempt to keep the hands steady, or a tendency to make your hands into tight fists, or to rest them on the horse's neck or withers, or to hold your breath: these are telltale signs that you are not entirely in balance.

Look, no reins

This exercise can be helpful for riders who tend to restrict the horse's head and neck with the rein contact, or use the reins to 'pick up' the horse on take-off when jumping, or to stand in the stirrups instead of folding.

Benefits

This exercise can be fun and a good confidence-giver. It teaches the rider to trust the horse and improves rider balance and position when jumping. It is helpful for those riders who tend to restrict the horse's head and neck with the rein contact, or use the reins to 'pick up' the horse on take-off, or to stand in the stirrups instead of folding.

How to do it

❏ Warm up on the flat first. You may also find it helpful to practise Exercise 48, Hovering trot.
❏ Knot the reins so that you can still use them to ride normally, but when you let go of them they will lie on your horse's neck without any risk of him getting a front foot caught through them.
❏ When you're ready to begin jumping, always start with a single upright. Using a correctly positioned placing pole in front of it can help produce a consistent, predictable take-off point each time. Approach the fence in a balanced and active trot, ensuring that you ride straight and towards the centre of it. Two or three strides away let go of the reins but keep your hands in a normal position.

❏ As the horse takes off and is in the air over the fence, push both hands forwards towards the horse's mouth. Alternatively, try pushing the hands down and forwards towards the horse's point of shoulder – this can help if you tend to get in front of the movement. Avoid pushing the hands along the horse's crest as this encourages you to lean on his neck for support, rather than developing a secure and independent position. It can also encourage you to get in front of the movement.
❏ On landing, take up the reins again two or three strides after the fence. Once you are confident jumping a single fence, add others to form a short grid. This will help you to work on improving your balance on landing and between fences as well as in the air over them.

DO: put a neckstrap or breastplate on the horse so that if you lose your balance, there is something to hold on to securely while you reorganize yourself.

AVOID: overdoing things. Jumping, especially gridwork, can be tiring for the horse and demanding on his concentration and he is likely to tire long before the rider does so.

SAFETY FIRST!

This exercise should only be attempted with a steady, reliable jumper that is not likely to rush or run out at the fences, and in a safe, enclosed area. An assistant will be needed to help set up and alter the fences; these do not need to be high.

TIP

Jumping spread fences can be helpful when working on position, as the horse spends more time in the air over them, which therefore also gives you more time to think about yourself.

Pacing

This is a TTouch rider exercise that will help you to coordinate hand and leg signals on each side and remove tension in the back and legs.

Benefits
This TTouch rider exercise sounds ridiculously simple, but it can be quite a test for some, really making you think about what you're doing. It helps increase your ability to coordinate hand and leg signals on each side. It can also help you in changing habits such as stiffening through the lower back and legs, which often happens if you normally ride a strong horse or one on its forehand.

How to do it
❏ When you walk you will usually tend to move the opposite hand and leg at the same time. Try walking instead swinging the arm on the same side as the leg which is moving.

DO: bend your knees as much as you would when walking normally – it's easy to end up moving in a straight-legged goose-step if you don't concentrate.

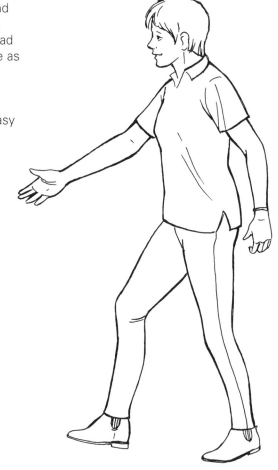

55

Opposite circles

This exercise helps improve control and coordination, and demonstrates how some apparently simple movements are in fact very demanding.

Benefits

This dismounted exercise can be quite challenging for many people and it may take a little while to master, as well as a great deal of concentration. However, it helps improve control and coordination, and gives you a healthy appreciation of how some movements, which on the surface seem very simple, can sometimes be very demanding for our horses.

How to do it

- ❏ Sit down and with your right foot draw a clockwise circle in the air.
- ❏ At the same time trace an anti-clockwise circle in the air with the index finger of your right hand. You'll probably find that at first, as you start making the anti-clockwise circle, your foot begins to change direction and to mimic what your hand is doing.
- ❏ Having mastered the exercise, try doing the reverse – circling your foot in an anti-clockwise direction and your finger in a clockwise one.
- ❏ Repeat with the left hand and foot.

DO: take it very slowly to begin with, as this will make it easier to succeed.

AVOID: giving up too quickly if you find it difficult initially – it is possible, and it is worth persevering.

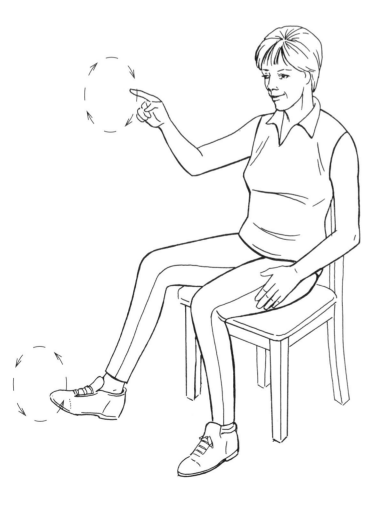

Pat head, rub tummy

Like the previous exercise, this one is also good for improving your coordination.

Benefits

This is another exercise to help improve your coordination and one with which you'll probably already be familiar, although not necessarily in connection with horses and riding!

How to do it

❏ Pat your head with your right hand and simultaneously rub your tummy with the left hand.

❏ Once you can do this, swap over hands so you are patting your head with your left hand and rubbing your tummy with the right one. It's likely that you'll find it easier to do one way round than the other, so this exercise can also help you to become less one-sided.

❏ Try increasing the difficulty by patting your head at a different speed to which you are rubbing your tummy.

DO: ask someone to hold your horse for you if you are doing this while mounted, although it's an exercise that can just as usefully be done without a horse.

AVOID: being over-vigorous – try to develop control and subtlety in your movements, so rub and pat gently.

EXERCISE

57

Super short stirrups

Riding with very short stirrups will make you appreciate how important it is to be in balance through the upper body. It will also stretch the calf muscles and help you let your weight down into your heels.

Benefits

Riding with very short stirrups will make you appreciate how important it is to be in balance through the upper body; even the slightest loss will be immediately noticeable. You should find yourself automatically wanting to sit taller. It will also stretch the calf muscles and help you let your weight down into your heels.

SAFETY FIRST!

Riding like this should only be attempted on a calm, steady horse that is known well to you, as it does place you in a precarious position.

How to do it

❏ Shorten your stirrups as much as you can without your knee sticking out over the front edge of the saddle flap.
❏ Get used to the feel in walk first and then try a little rising trot.
❏ This can be a surprisingly tiring exercise, so you should do it for only a few minutes at a time.

DO: use the horse's mane to help you maintain your balance when necessary.

AVOID: allowing your seat to be pushed towards the back of the saddle; try to maintain it in the central, deepest part.

Touching toes

Besides developing balance and coordination, this exercise will increase the rider's confidence and also improve waist suppleness and stomach muscle tone.

Benefits

This exercise has multiple benefits in that it helps build confidence as well as balance and coordination. It also increases waist suppleness and gives the stomach muscles a workout at the same time. For younger children it can be a fun and effective way to learn the left/near and right/off sides, especially when made more complex and challenging by asking them to touch a toe with the opposite hand. Together with touching other parts of the pony's body and saddle, it can be made into a game along the lines of 'Simon says' so that they also learn to identify simple parts of the equine anatomy and saddle.

TEACHING SAFETY TIP

Be careful that younger children don't lose their balance in their enthusiasm to show what they can do – keep a steadying hand on their foot and stirrup.

How to do it

❑ Keep your feet in the stirrups, and either hold the reins in one hand or knot them, letting them lie on the horse's neck.
❑ With your free hand, reach down to touch the toe on the same side.
❑ Sit up again, raising your free hand up in the air above your head as you do so.
❑ Reach down to touch the opposite toe with your hand.
❑ Repeat up to five times and then repeat with the other hand.
❑ When you are feeling confident enough, try the same exercise with one arm folded behind your back; doing it like this keeps your back flatter and your hips squarer to the saddle.

DO: reach as far as you can, but don't compromise your security to do so. If necessary, hold the neckstrap or a lock of mane with one hand for support.

AVOID: drawing the lower leg back or pushing it forwards, lifting the foot or gripping up with the heel. Try to maintain a correct and stable leg position with slightly lowered heels and to keep the seat as straight in the saddle as possible.

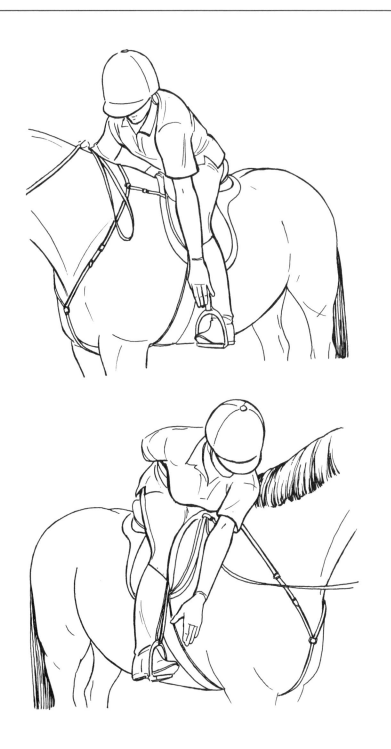

13

'FEEL'

'Never before have I felt such a horse between my knees.'

Arthur Conan Doyle 1859–1930: British author, poet and doctor

THE EXERCISES

'Feel' is an elusive ability for many riders. Primarily it is the ability to know what the horse's body is doing through the physical sensations registered by the hands, legs, seat and back. The better developed this faculty, the better able the rider is to determine whether the horse is going correctly, to note improvements and responses to his own actions and to apply aids at the most advantageous moment.

But developing 'feel' isn't solely about registering how the horse is moving. It's also about increasing your own body self-awareness. As this improves it becomes easier to identify problem areas in your position, to make corrections and note the difference between 'before' and 'after'. As your own awareness grows, so does your sensitivity to your horse's movement.

Recognizing bad habits

This is more challenging than it might sound, as our bodies can be very good at fooling us, sending false feedback to our brains. You may be absolutely convinced that you are sitting straight for example, but when somebody adjusts your position so that you are truly sitting with your weight more equally distributed across the saddle, it can feel terrible and as though you are now about to slide off to one side. Sometimes it's only by seeing the evidence on film that you can actually believe what you're being told, and changing to a new, more correct posture can feel very 'wrong' at first, even though it's correct.

This is due to 'muscle memory' – familiar patterns of movement that are established through being done on a regular basis over a period of time. The more frequently that an action is repeated, the more deeply implanted it becomes and the easier to repeat it. It enables you to walk, brush your teeth, comb your hair or (with enough practice) type without having to apply much conscious thought to the processes actually involved beyond a desire to do them.

How to correct bad habits

But this can work against you, since unfortunately it is as easy to learn bad habits as good ones, which then become part of the muscle memory. The more ingrained these patterns of movement become, the more difficult it is to alter them, both physically and mentally. Changes to what is familiar can feel uncomfortable and 'wrong', and the muscles will want to revert back to what they perceive as being correct. This will tend to happen every time you stop consciously thinking about it until such time as the new posture is established.

Trying to 'unlearn' bad habits that have crept in unnoticed can be deeply frustrating and time-consuming. It can also be more difficult than learning and practising correct ones right from the start, hence the importance of good teaching for novice riders, who should then continue having regular lessons throughout their riding career.

59

Bareback riding

This exercise can help improve your balance and straightness, and it will help those riders with tight leg muscles. You will also be more 'in tune' with the horse mentally and physically.

Benefits

Without a saddle between you and your horse, you'll be able to feel what's happening beneath you more easily; you may begin to notice even quite subtle things you hadn't been aware of previously, such as the movement of the horse's ribcage as he breathes. This new awareness will continue to develop even when the saddle is back in place again. With no saddle or stirrups for support, this exercise also helps improve your balance. You become more in tune mentally as well as physically with the horse, whilst the warmth of his back and sides can help relax tight leg muscles, too. Ultimately bareback riding can also be a great confidence booster, provided it is sensibly introduced.

SAFETY FIRST!

Bareback riding should not cause any problems as long as it is approached sensibly. Always use a quiet, sensible horse, not one that is likely to be spooky or excitable, and work in a safe, enclosed area.

How to do it

❑ Either get a leg-up or use a mounting block, as this will be less disturbing for the horse. Sit slightly further forward than you would in a saddle; you'll find that your seat automatically tends to migrate into the right place.

❑ Don't be in a hurry to move off; spend a minute or two in halt, simply getting used to the feel. If possible, get someone to lead you, as this allows you to concentrate on yourself and what your horse is doing without you being distracted by the need to control him as well. Your assistant should lead him from a headcollar worn under the bridle, because this ensures there is no interference with the bit, which might inhibit head and shoulder movement. Leave the reins slack because this allows the horse's head and neck to move freely, giving you a greater degree of feedback. It's also a good way of finding out how much you rely on the rein contact for support.

❑ When you're ready, move off into walk, noting the movement you can feel, not just in your horse's back, but also in his ribcage, shoulders and neck. You will probably also find yourself becoming much more aware of the action of his hind legs, and better able to discern which one is moving. Try some turns and circles, feeling how his ribcage and your legs come more into contact and how this affects your straightness.

❏ Vary the speed of the walk and introduce some transitions to halt as well. You should find yourself becoming increasingly aware of just how important balance is, as well as the presence of any stiffness or crookedness within your body, which interferes with this. You should also discover that your legs maintain a more constant, but softer contact with your horse's sides.

❏ If you find yourself slipping to one side while walking in a straight line, it may be due to a habit of sitting crookedly, but which manages to escape your attention when you can use the stirrups to help compensate. Avoid gripping with your legs as this will make you stiffen and increase the sideways slide. Straighten yourself so your weight is equally distributed across the horse's back, then allow your legs to relax and let gravity help draw them downwards.

DO: use a neckstrap if the mane is thin or short, so you have something you can hold on to should you start to lose your balance or begin to slip to one side.

AVOID: suffering in silence if the horse has very high withers or a prominent backbone. Use a securely fitted saddlepad.

Moving on

This exercise can often be a good way of helping to improve sitting to the trot, but only introduce the trot when you feel confident in walk. Return to walk again the moment you start to slip or lose your balance. It doesn't need to be very active – a slow, gentle jog trot is quite sufficient and will encourage you to remain relaxed and supple through your back, rather than bracing stiffly against the movement.

Eyes wide shut

This exercise teaches you to listen properly to the horse and improves your 'feel' for what he is doing so that your aids may be more appropriate and better timed.

Benefits

This is an exercise in which you remain fairly passive, which sounds easy, but can be more challenging than you might imagine. Without realizing it, many riders tend to be quite 'busy', often unnecessarily so. Simply sitting quietly, doing nothing more than absorbing, mentally and physically, all the sensations of the horse's movement, can feel quite strange and the temptation to provide some input difficult to resist. As much as anything else, it is a lesson in learning to listen properly to your horse. Without mastering this skill, your 'feel' for what the horse is doing and your ability to apply an appropriate and correctly timed action that is based on this information, will always be limited.

How to do it

❏ While your horse is being led or lunged, place the reins in one hand and place two fingers of the other under the front arch of the saddle.
❏ While the horse is moving in walk, shut both eyes. You should find that without any visual distractions you become much more aware of how the horse is moving. You may even be surprised at just how much movement there is – not just up and down and backwards and forwards, but also from side to side.
❏ Gradually you will find yourself also becoming aware of the movement of the horse's shoulders and each individual limb, his ribcage beneath your legs and even his breathing.

❏ When you feel confident to do so, try letting go of the front of the saddle, knot the reins and let them lie on the horse's neck. Allow your arms to either hang down by your sides, or carry them as though you were holding reins.
❏ You can incorporate this with some of the other exercises here, such as counting the footfalls, or calling out 'left' and 'right' as each hind foot moves forwards.

DO: try to maintain as correct a posture as possible. Being passive is not the same as slumping in the saddle and becoming a dead weight for your horse to carry!

AVOID: squeezing your eyes tightly shut because this will make you tighten through the jaw and neck.

Moving on

Provided you feel confident, establish a steady, regular trot while you are being led or lunged and then try shutting your eyes again.

SAFETY FIRST!

Never ride with your eyes closed unless your horse is calm and sensible and a competent person is available to lead or lunge him. If at any time you start to feel dizzy, open your eyes and tell the person leading or lungeing you so they can halt the horse until you feel all right again.

Trotting diagonals

Recognizing which diagonal you are on can help develop your feel for how the horse is moving and how to coordinate your actions with those of the horse.

Benefits

Changing the trotting diagonal each time you change the rein helps to minimize one-sidedness and unequal muscular development in your horse. Working out which diagonal you are on can also be a useful exercise in developing your sense of feel for how the horse is moving beneath you. You can also begin to learn to coordinate and correctly time your actions with those of the horse.

TIP

You might be inclined to forget about diagonals when hacking out, but it's still important to try and spend a similar amount of time on each diagonal.

How to do it
❏ Establish rising to the trot.
❏ Without using peripheral vision or looking down, try to decide which diagonal you are on; then confirm whether you are correct by looking. Change to the correct diagonal (sitting as your horse's outside shoulder moves back towards you) if you are working in the school and are on the wrong one.
❏ Return to sitting to the trot for a few strides, then start rising again and once more decide which diagonal you are on.
❏ When you become more proficient, try to start rising at the moment that will put you on to the correct diagonal straightaway.

DO: aim for a regular and active gait, as this makes it easier to determine which diagonal you are on and to change it if you wish. In the case of very one-sided horses with a distinct preference, it also makes it more difficult for them to throw you to their favoured diagonal.

AVOID: looking down! Use peripheral vision instead to check which diagonal you're on. If you really do need to take more of a look than this, make it no more than a quick glance and then look up again. If necessary use Exercise 9 Head stretch to help regain a good head and neck posture.

Moving on
Most horses prefer one diagonal to the other. Try riding for a few strides on one diagonal, then change to the other one and compare the regularity and freedom of movement when on the more comfortable diagonal with the other rein.

TIP

The sitting phase of rising to the trot is the best time to close your legs and ask for more impulsion – you will be more effective and your position less likely to be disturbed.

Canter leads

Whether your interest is dressage or jumping, not having to look down and check on your horse's canter lead is really helpful. If you can keep looking ahead you will be much better able to rebalance him, engage his quarters and ride accurately.

Benefits

This is a progression from the trotting diagonal exercise. Being able to tell by feel which canter lead your horse is on is necessary both for dressage work and for jumping. Looking ahead ensures you are ready for the next fence, able to rebalance your horse, engage his quarters and ride more accurately towards it. Looking down to check on your canter lead when landing after a fence can make you collapse forwards into an insecure position should your horse stumble. This makes it hard for him to recover, pushing him on to his forehand and increasing the likelihood of this happening. And if you are jumping a combination or fences set at a related distance, it can also affect the striding.

How to do it

❏ Each time that you ask your horse to canter, try to determine which canter lead your horse is on without actually looking. Once you have decided, use your peripheral vision or

glance quickly down at the shoulders – the one that is moving the furthest forwards will be the leading leg. You will also have a sensation of your outside seatbone sliding diagonally towards the inside one.

❏ Make the exercise more demanding by asking for canter from a straight line, rather than in a corner or from a circle. Without the curvature of a corner or circle to aid you, your canter aids and preparation will need to become more correct and precise.

❏ As well as helping to improve your communication, this exercise further develops your 'feel', as you will begin to become aware of how your horse feels when he is correctly positioned to take a specific canter lead.

Moving on

You may apply the exercise to jumping as well. Ride towards and away from a fence on a straight line, determining which canter lead the horse is on as he moves away from the fence.

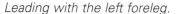
Leading with the left foreleg.

How does it feel?

This exercise increases your awareness of your horse's movement and encourages you to analyse your own actions more critically.

Benefits

Like Exercise 60 Eyes wide shut, this is very much about 'listening' and feeling properly what your horse is doing. It is also beneficial to describe what you are doing in response, because this engages your brain and you analyse everything that's going on, rather than just reacting mechanically to it.

How to do it

❏ You can do this exercise on your own, but it's often fun to take it in turns with a friend. Not only can you provide feedback on each other's efforts, but it can be helpful in developing your powers of observation when lungeing or working in hand.

❏ While walking, trotting and cantering, describe what your horse is doing in as much detail as possible – not just including what gait he is in, but whether he feels comfortable, bouncy, balanced, lopsided, active, lazy, responsive, taking a level contact, and so on. Once you start you'll be surprised at just how much there is to talk about, and it'll help you to become more discerning as to the quality of work with a greater awareness of the areas that need working on.

Moving on

Next, try including details of what you are doing, as this makes you consciously take stock of your position and aids, and in particular of any undesirable 'knee-jerk' responses to the horse's actions, such as pulling in response to him leaning on the bit. It's also an excellent way of analysing whether what you are doing is helping or even necessary; it's surprisingly easy to settle into a habitual pattern of actions, such as a constant nagging with the legs or hands without being aware of it.

64

Gym ball

This is an effective way to develop straightness and to encourage better posture through your torso.

Benefits

A gym ball can be bought quite cheaply and is a great way of helping to develop your sense of straightness – something which isn't easy to do when mounted and without someone on the ground to help you. As it is hard to slouch when sitting on a gym ball, it will also encourage better posture through your torso. You may find it helpful to sit on it in front of a mirror initially so you can relate what you see to what you are feeling. Once you've got the feel and can sit in an easy, balanced position, you can sit on it while watching television or reading. A gym ball can also be used for various strengthening, toning, stretching and suppling exercises, so will have more than one purpose.

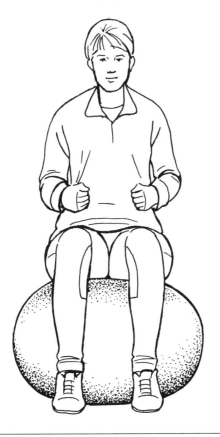

How to do it

❏ Sit on the centre of the ball with both feet flat on the floor at about shoulder width apart and with your knees in line above your ankles. Keep your body vertical, using the abdominal and back muscles to support your posture.

❏ You may be surprised at how difficult this apparently simple exercise is. You will immediately become aware of any crookedness as you'll find it hard to balance and stay on the ball. It will help you to appreciate how much you may usually use your arms and legs to compensate for lack of straightness or a tendency to collapse, as you will be tempted to move them around to help you balance. Pay attention to the correct alignment of your head, as this will help (see Chapter 5).

❏ When you're sitting in perfect balance you'll find it fairly effortless to keep the ball between yourself and the ground. When you transfer this same ability to the saddle, you'll find riding less tiring for both you and your horse, and it will be easier to apply clear, independent hand and leg aids.

DO: deflate the ball slightly if you find this exercise difficult, as it will be more stable until you've developed a better balance and posture as well as a little more strength in the abdominal and lower back muscles.

AVOID: leaning forwards or trying to hunch up, as this will make things worse.

Moving on

Once you can sit on the ball in good balance, try practising seat and back aids. This will help you learn to develop subtlety in their use, to avoid stiffening, and to appreciate how even the smallest of movements can create a big effect.

Which one when?

Getting to know the sequence of the horse's legs at each gait will help you to apply the aids at the correct moment and to develop a better feel for rhythm and tempo.

Benefits

Knowing what each of your horse's legs is doing will stand you in good stead in helping you to time aid application for best effect – when performing lateral work for example, or asking for a canter strike-off or a flying change. Learning to identify the movement of the legs will also help you detect inequalities in strength, stride length and flexion between them, and to develop a better feel for regularity of rhythm and tempo.

How to do it

❏ Starting with the halt, analyse the way in which your horse is standing. Does it feel as though he is absolutely four square, or has he left a leg behind? How are the front legs positioned? Consider whether he is balanced, too.

Is he supporting his weight equally over all four legs, or tending to lean forwards over the front legs? Once you have decided, ask your assistant to tell you how they look.
❏ Ride several halt/walk transitions. Which leg moves first as your horse goes into walk – and is it the same leg each time?
❏ Count out the movement of the front legs, calling out 'left', 'right' as each moves in turn. Next, do the same with the hind legs – this is more difficult, and it's easy to get distracted and influenced by the movement of the shoulders. As well as being aware of which leg is moving at any moment, also pay attention to the regularity of each step.

❏ Finally, count all four footfalls of the walk. Do this out loud because it gives you a better sense of the rhythm. It's also a good way of improving your breathing if you're inclined to hold your breath when you are concentrating.

DO: count out loudly enough that your assistant can hear you, so he can check that you are counting the steps as they are actually happening, not when you think they should be happening.

Moving on

When ready, you can also try counting the movements of single legs, pairs of legs and complete sequences of leg movements in trot and canter.

TIP

Ask someone on the ground to watch and give you feedback when you ask, so you don't disturb your horse's balance by leaning to one side to try and see for yourself what his legs are doing.

BREATHING

'… if I feel myself unfit to ride my horse, I stop …'

Michel de Montaigne 1533–1592: French philosopher, statesman, author

THE EXERCISES

Breathing is something we all tend to take for granted and often don't think a great deal about in connection with riding, but it can have a direct impact on your position. Any physical activity increases the body's requirement for oxygen and the rate of breathing accordingly becomes faster to meet the demand. Poor breathing technique, however, as much as a lack of cardiovascular fitness, can lead to getting out of breath quickly, which in riding will lead to poor posture and stiffness in addition to feelings of fatigue.

Tension in the body

Respiration will also increase if you're feeling nervous or excited – it's part of a natural and instinctive response by your body to prepare it for 'fight or flight'. Concentrating hard on what you are doing is another time when your normal breathing pattern often becomes disrupted. Whether you are holding your breath in an effort to get something right, or breathing rapidly and shallowly through nervousness, the outcome is the same: tension is created within your body, making you stiff, abrupt and uncoordinated, affecting your security in the saddle and your ability to communicate effectively with your horse.

Horses are very observant of, and sensitive to, sound, touch and body language, and undesirable rapid and shallow breathing will indicate to them that you are feeling stressed. They will then begin to look round for the source of your anxiety, and in the same way will ready themselves for flight or fight.

Releasing tension

Just as the way you are feeling can influence the way you breathe, the reverse is equally true. Everyone can alter their breathing patterns, and through them release tension, relaxing both body and mind. Not surprisingly, many ancient traditions such as yoga and meditation make use of special breathing techniques in order to alter mental states and help spiritual development.

The exercises here are aimed at promoting efficient breathing and calmness as well as reducing tension, which will help reduce stiffness and enable you to achieve a better position. In addition, deeper, rhythmical breathing will communicate a sense of calmness and relaxation to your horse.

BREATHE OUT DURING TRANSITIONS!

When asking your horse to increase or decrease gait or gait speed, it's instinctive to take a deep breath in preparation for the increased physical effort of getting him to speed up or slow down. Consequently this can make you stiff and lacking in subtlety in your aid application, and depending on his temperament, the effect on your horse may be either to make him resistant to your request, or to rush forwards out of balance. Try doing the opposite, and as you ask for transitions between or within a gait, breathe out instead. With just a few consistent repetitions you should find your horse becoming more responsive to your softer, subtler, calmer, more comfortable and better coordinated posture and aids. This can be especially effective when slowing down and when asking for halt.

Deep breathing

Practise this exercise dismounted first of all so there is nothing to distract you. Then try it in halt while mounted at the beginning of a work session, or at any time when you feel stressed or anxious.

Benefits

Breathing deeply using your diaphragm is more efficient than shallow upper chest breathing. Each inhalation and exhalation fills and empties the lungs more completely. This means more oxygen is available to the body and there is less build-up of waste products, so you'll tire less rapidly. Developing a deeper breathing technique will also enable you to be a more relaxed and coordinated rider, better able to maintain and effect postural corrections and in addition can be used to reduce any feelings of anxiety and stress. Practise this dismounted first of all so you have no distractions and then try it in halt whilst mounted at the beginning of a work session, or at any time when you feel stressed or anxious.

How to do it

❑ Sitting in a chair, place one hand on your abdomen, positioned just below your navel, so you are consciously breathing from lower down.
❑ Breathe in deeply through your nose, counting to ten. Let the breath push your hand out.
❑ Hold your breath for a count of five.
❑ Release your breath slowly between your lips, counting to ten as you do so.
❑ Repeat five times.

DO: sit up straight; slouching will affect your ability to breathe deeply.

AVOID: holding your breath by pressing your lips tightly together. Allow them to be slightly parted and think about your diaphragm helping to hold the air in your lungs instead.

TIP

If you can remember to breathe out, breathing in will take care of itself!

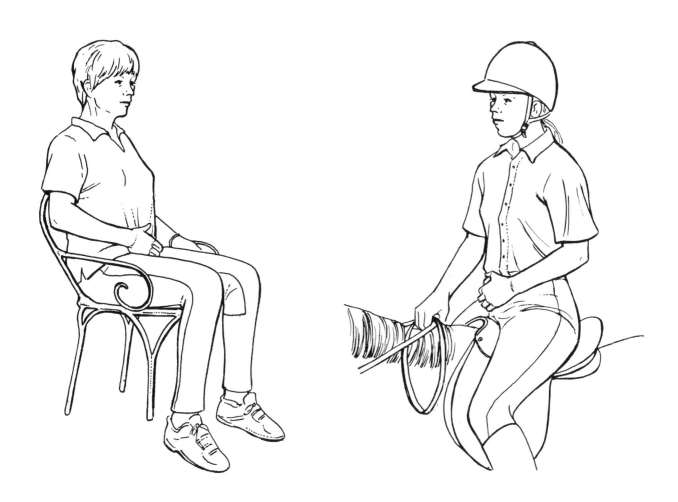

67

Improving breathing and posture

This exercise will help improve both posture and breathing.

Benefits

Slumping through your torso and/or rounding or hunching your shoulders will have a direct, adverse influence on the way you breathe. This exercise combines improving posture and breathing. It will help you to feel the difference when the movement of the ribcage isn't being inhibited and can expand more completely. It will also encourage you to focus on breathing deeply and steadily, using as much lung capacity as possible.

How to do it

❑ Stand with your feet slightly apart and your arms hanging in a relaxed way by your sides.
❑ As you slowly breathe in, gradually raise your arms out to the sides at the same time, coordinating their movement so that by the time your lungs feel full, your arms are vertical above your head.
❑ Hold for a count of five.
❑ Slowly breathe out through your mouth, whilst slowly lowering your arms, again coordinating the movement so they reach their original starting position as you finish exhaling.
❑ Repeat five times.

DO: allow your shoulders to relax as you lower your arms. Beware of allowing tension to creep in through the back of your neck.

AVOID: allowing your torso to slump again as your arms return to your sides.

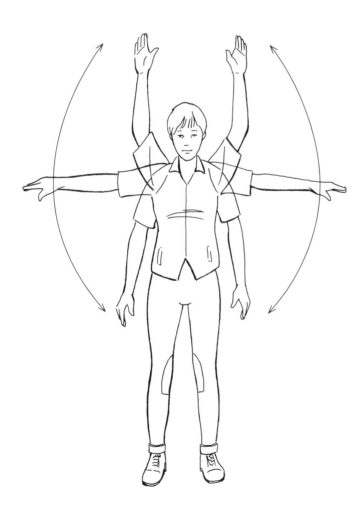

Chatterbox

Some riders hold their breath unintentionally, particularly when jumping, which makes for stiffness in position. This exercise in talking will help you breathe more regularly and so ease any tension.

Benefits

Sometimes you may not actually realize that you are breathing irregularly or incorrectly. Talking or singing to your horse while riding is a very simple and easy way of checking, as well as helping you to learn to breathe regularly while actually working your horse.

How to do it

❑ It doesn't matter whether you talk or sing – whichever you prefer. Some riders like to use a kind of mantra, such as repeating multiplication tables, or the days of the week.

❑ Consciously note how you are singing or talking. It should be phrased naturally, not with one word running into another, or a lot of words gabbled out, followed by a pause while you take another deep breath, ready for the next sentence. This is a sure sign that you are inclined to hold your breath. Improve your speaking/singing phrasing and your breathing in turn will become more regular meaning that you will have less tendency to run out of breath.

❑ Many riders tend to hold their breath when jumping in anticipation of the take-off in front of a fence. This makes for a stiff position, often out of synchronization with the horse's movements, and can cause the horse to take off too early. When jumping a course of fences, the rider is frequently out of breath and panting on reaching the end of it! Counting the strides on the approach to a fence can be a useful exercise to help keep you breathing in a rhythmical way, and has the added bonus of helping you to 'get your eye in for a stride' – that is, learning to judge the distance you are from the take-off point in front of a fence.

❑ Note that counting the number of strides as you approach – one, two, three, four – is preferable to doing a countdown (four, three, two, one), because if you get it wrong and there is actually room for one or even more strides than you anticipated, it's then quite easy to freeze and hold your breath, which defeats the whole object of the exercise.

❑ Continue to keep speaking by saying 'take-off', 'flight' and 'landing' through these phases, and then carry on counting strides as you ride away from the fence.

DO: make sure you are counting the strides your horse is taking as he takes them, and are not just counting out of sequence with his limb movement.

EMOTIONAL ISSUES

'The one great precept and practice in using a horse is this – never deal with him when you are in a fit of passion.'

Xenophon 431–353BC: Greek soldier, historian, author

THE EXERCISES

When we're feeling happy, an upbeat mood tends to have a direct and positive effect on everything we do – difficult or demanding things seem to be much easier to achieve and we're more likely to be successful in attaining our goals. In a darker mood we're more likely to be negative and to make mistakes, be less confident and therefore less likely to succeed.

Mood can also have a direct effect on posture. Visualize the body language of an angry person – clenched jaw muscles, rapid breathing, clenched fists, tense shoulders – and then someone who is anxious or fearful – shoulders hunched defensively, head ducked down between them. Their emotions are apparent in their posture. Such emotional responses can cause our position to deteriorate and it will be much harder to correct it. Furthermore, our body will betray our feelings to our horse, who may become reactive as a result.

The emotions most likely to affect our riding are frustration/irritation/anger, and anxiety/apprehension/fear. These may be directly related to our riding activities, or be present as a result of other, unconnected events. Whatever the cause, it's important to recognize their existence in order to do something about it.

Anger management

Some days things just don't go according to plan and one of the worst things you can do is to lose your temper. Your horse will pick up on your tension through your deteriorating posture and communication, and is liable to become stressed himself.

When you feel yourself losing control of your emotions, you need to stop before you do something you may regret later; if necessary, dismount and put your horse away. However, you may find that it's enough just to 'take a deep breath', as in the old adage. Breathing can play an important part in helping with anger management, and doing the breathing exercises suggested in Chapter 14 is an excellent way of releasing tension and regaining some of your mental and physical equilibrium.

Other things you can try to ensure you don't lose your cool include the following:

❏ picking up on your bad vibes is more likely to make your horse reactive, so if you've had a stressful day don't go near him until you've got rid of some of that stress – try yoga exercises, meditation, or some vigorous occupation such as sweeping the yard – whichever works best for you

❏ if you are encountering a riding problem, don't feel you have to battle it out on your own – seek help from an experienced teacher instead

❏ be realistic in the goals you set yourself and your horse. Expecting too much will certainly lead to frustration when you fail to achieve them, and even if you don't lose your temper, you're likely to be much tougher on the horse than is fair. Try to notice the small improvements instead of always looking for big ones so you can find lots of reasons for rewarding him and giving yourself a pat on the back. This will help to keep negative feelings and actions at bay.

Fear

The outer physical signs of inner mental stress are unmistakable and unpleasant: racing heart, dry mouth, butterflies in your tummy, clammy palms. All sorts of things can make you feel anxious or even downright terrified, such as:

❑ riding a different horse for the first time
❑ attending a new riding school
❑ taking an examination
❑ jumping
❑ hacking out
❑ remounting after a fall.

Whatever the cause, it inevitably affects your riding adversely, as well as making you think less clearly and logically, and you are likely to be stiff and tense in your posture. How you tackle the problem will vary according to each individual and their circumstances – different things work better for some people than others.

The following might help:

❑ as with frustration or anger, deep breathing will help to relax and calm you; if feeling nervous, it's very likely you will either be holding your breath, or breathing shallowly and rapidly. Try the suggested breathing exercises in Chapter 14
❑ depending on whether it makes your nerves better or worse, encourage friends and family either to be present to lend their support or to stay at home
❑ avoid alcohol to calm your nerves – it's more likely to make them worse and can also adversely affect your balance, coordination and judgment

❑ many riders have found Neuro Linguistic Programming (NLP) very helpful. It analyses the reasons why you may be feeling nervous and seeks to replace your unwanted negative thoughts and feelings with positive ones
❑ if your nerves stem from not being entirely sure what to do in certain situations, or from doubting your ability to cope, ask an experienced and sympathetic teacher for advice and practical help
❑ don't be pressured by others into doing things for which you don't feel ready. It is one thing to stretch yourself a little in order to progress and quite another to feel real apprehension. This may well affect your ability to succeed, which will then sap your confidence further
❑ do some stretching and suppling exercises in areas where you are conscious of tension – just as the mind can affect the way you hold your body, so making changes to body posture can help to alter emotions
❑ some people find Bach flower remedies or aromatherapy oils of help in soothing frayed nerves and restoring balance to mind and body.
❑ TTouch (see Chapter 1 The basics, Learning tools, for more information) can also help in combating nerves – try the two exercises that are suggested in this section.

Competition nerves

Nervousness is frequently experienced when competing and can, to a degree, actually be an asset, helping to increase focus and determination. If nerves start to get out of hand, however, then far from giving your performance a winning edge they can cause you to psych yourself out. They can also directly affect your position for the worse and your anxiety will be communicated to your horse. This will adversely affect both the way he moves and behaves.

The exercises and other suggestions given in this chapter will all help. Other things you can do to help keep nerves to a minimum include the following:

❏ enter classes at a level with which you feel comfortable and confident – preferably lower than the one you are working at when at home

❏ play some soothing classical music while travelling to the show so you arrive feeling calm; you can continue to hum the tunes to yourself (and your horse) while preparing for your class

❏ try to keep yourself occupied doing things such as rolling bandages, sprucing your horse up, or checking the course or test, so you give your mind and body something else to do apart from being nervous

❏ take along a puzzle book with crosswords, sudoku and other brainteasers if you have entered several classes and know there'll be spare time in between them. This will give you something to focus on and is more likely to engage your attention than a book or magazine.

If the following three exercises suggested sound a little far-fetched, think for a moment about the gestures that an anxious or nervous person makes; very often they'll either tug at an ear, touch or chew at the upper lip, or wring their hands. These are subconscious gestures by the body to help restore calm. Using the TTouch exercises will allow you to do this in a more effective way.

TTouch mouthwork

Use this exercise if you are starting to lose your temper or if you are feeling particularly nervous.

Benefits

Using TTouches around your mouth can be helpful if you are nervous. In particular the place just beneath the nasal septum has a direct connection with the limbic system in the brain which controls emotions, and working it can be calming. If you feel your temper becoming frayed, it may help to take a little time to think about your breathing and to do this exercise, since jaw muscles are likely to become tight at such moments.

How to do it

❑ Use the tips or pads of your fingers to make small circles around your mouth.
❑ If you're inclined to clench your teeth together when tense, do these little TTouches around the lower jaw, cheeks and cheekbones as well to help relax these areas.

DO: use only just enough pressure to move the skin, keeping your fingers slightly curved and your wrists soft and supple. With both earwork and mouthwork, perform the movements very slowly, otherwise they will have the opposite effect from calming you.

AVOID: being in a hurry. Be aware of the fact that when stressed or feeling under pressure, you'll be inclined to do things much faster than you realize. See if you can make each slide and circular TTouch last for two to three seconds. You may be surprised at just how slow you perceive this to be when you are feeling on edge.

TTouch earwork

This exercise will have a calming effect as long as it is done slowly. Done too quickly and it will do the opposite!

Benefits
Earwork is a quick way of helping to alleviate both the tight feeling in your tummy and the elevated breathing that is caused by nerves.

How to do it
❑ Taking one ear between a thumb and slightly curled forefinger, gently stroke from the inner to outside edges.
❑ Move the position of your thumb and finger slightly each time until the whole area of the ear has been covered by your strokes.
❑ Having worked on one ear, do the other one, but don't try and do both at the same time.

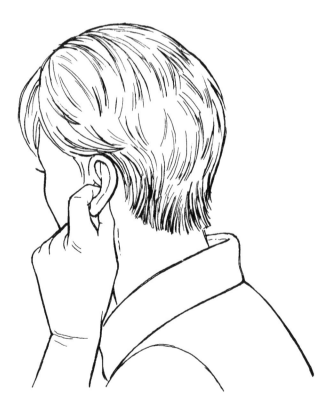

Acupoints

Using acupoints has a calming effect and will reduce feelings of fear and anxiety.

Benefits

You can try using one or two of the following acupoints at times when you are feeling stressed and anxious:

❏ **P6 (Inner Gate)** – located on the underside of the wrist, between the tendons, approximately two and a half finger-widths back towards your body from the middle of the crease in your wrist: this helps to reduce fear

❏ **Ht7 (Spirit's Gate)** – found on the little finger side of the wrist at the wrist crease where there is a small groove between the main ulna (forearm bone) and the tendon: this has a calming effect

❏ **SI 3–4** – rub along the outer edge of your hand where the skin pattern changes, from the base of the little finger along to the wrist crease: this reduces anxiety.

How to do it

With the exception of SI 3–4:

❏ place the tip of your thumb directly on the acupoint at an angle of 90 degrees

❏ add a little gentle pressure

❏ hold each acupoint for 30–60 seconds.

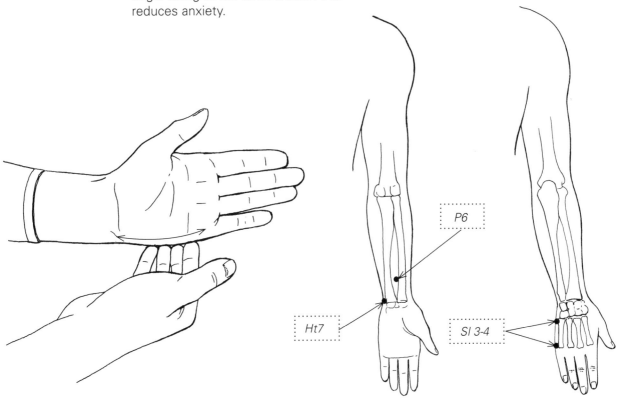

IMPROVING REIN CONTACT

'… you must refrain from pulling at his mouth with the bit as well as from spurring and whipping him. Most people think this is the way to make him look fine; but they only produce an effect exactly contrary to what they desire …'

Xenophon 431–353BC: Greek soldier, historian, author

THE EXERCISES

Although the exercises in this chapter will help you to improve the subtlety, sensitivity and proficiency of your rein management, it's important not to forget that ultimately the quality of the rein contact relies upon maintaining a correct riding position involving an independent seat in the saddle.

Knuckle to knuckle

This exercise can help you to develop a more consistent, yet sympathetic rein contact, and gain a greater understanding of how tensions in other areas affect rein contact and will help in making corrections.

Benefits

This is helpful in improving the ability to coordinate the movement of the hands, both for the person in the active role as well as for the passive partner. The exercise is also very useful for learning how to develop a more consistent, yet elastic rein contact.

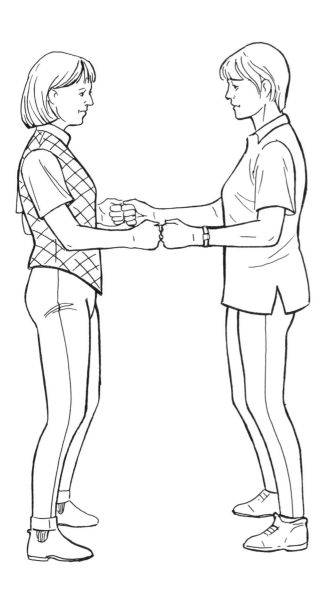

How to do it

❏ Stand facing your partner, feet spread comfortably apart with your weight evenly distributed over them, and knees slightly flexed.
❏ Begin with upper arms hanging by your sides, elbows flexed, forearms parallel to the ground and hands making soft fists, as though you were holding reins.
❏ Stand close enough to each other that you can lightly touch knuckles. Agree who is to be the 'active' person and who will be 'passive'; the active person moves first, one hand slowly backwards and forwards, then the other hand, and then moves both hands simultaneously, constantly varying the direction and degree of movement so that it is difficult to predict.
❏ The passive person tries to maintain the same light pressure against the active person's knuckles – neither losing contact, nor increasing it.
❏ Take it in turns to swap roles.

DO: give each other feedback while doing the exercise, as it's helpful in understanding how tensions and stiffness in other areas affect rein contact and aid in making corrections.

AVOID: holding your breath, biting your lip or tightening through the jaw as you concentrate on following your partner's actions. This will create tension in your neck and shoulders, and this will affect your ability to maintain that light knuckle-to-knuckle contact.

Bridle exchange

When it's your turn to be 'horse' you will find out how the smallest of movements is noticeable, and will gradually become more discerning as to which parts of the body are responsible. You will also notice how the rein contact affects the rest of the 'horse's' posture.

Benefits

Putting yourself at the other end of the reins for a change will help keep you motivated whenever you find enthusiasm for working on your overall posture beginning to flag.

How to do it

You'll need to pair up with a friend for this exercise – take it in turn to be 'horse' and 'rider'. It allows you to experience at first hand a little of what the horse feels, and can provide an insight as to why problems with rein contact and bit acceptance so often occur. At the same time you can receive constructive verbal feedback from your partner to help make you aware of particular faults, for example such as a dominant, heavy hand.

❏ Whichever of you is going to be the 'horse' wears the bridle, placing the headpiece and browband on top of the head and lightly looping two fingers of each hand through the bit rings on each side. This will give a good idea of how the rein contact has an effect not just on the mouth, but elsewhere in the horse's head and neck too, via the bridle. The 'rider' stands in front of the 'horse' holding the reins in both hands, feet spread comfortably apart and knees slightly flexed.

❏ Whoever is the 'rider' can be holding the reins with different hand positions and body postures:
  ❏ high/low/uneven
  ❏ hands close together/wide apart
  ❏ with stiff fingers
  ❏ with hunched shoulders
  ❏ collapsing through one side of the waist
  ❏ leaning backwards/forwards
  ❏ with rounded/hollow wrists
  ❏ in a correct position
  ❏ hollowing and stiffening through the back
  ❏ locking leg joints.

❏ Try different rein actions, too:
  ❏ pulling
  ❏ jerking
  ❏ keeping up a constant strong tension on both reins/ just one rein
  ❏ having a slightly slack rein
  ❏ making gentle squeezing actions with the fingers
  ❏ asking for halts and turns.

❏ The 'horse' can try the exercise with closed eyes, so there is no element of anticipation. Not knowing what sort of rein action is likely to happen next can be surprisingly worrying and makes you appreciate the depth of trust that horses, unable to predict the next move either, constantly place in us. It will also become noticeable how the rein contact affects the rest of the 'horse's' posture, whether it feels pleasant, uncomfortable or painful – and the same applies to the real thing.

❏ Throughout the exercise, whoever is 'horse' gives feedback to the 'rider', commenting on how it feels to be on the receiving end and in particular when something feels comfortable and pleasant. Take it in turns, and be subtle in your actions as 'rider' too. When it's your turn to be 'horse' you'll find how the smallest of movements is noticed, and you will gradually become more discerning as to which parts of the body are responsible.

74

The swan

This exercise is based on a Feldenkrais movement and is often used by trainee TTouch practitioners to improve coordination, precision and delicacy of action.

Benefits

This exercise is helpful for riders because it promotes flexibility in the neck and upper body, improves coordination, increases suppleness in the wrists and produces greater subtlety in your movements – all things that are fundamental in improving the quality of your contact. If you have neck or back problems, do the exercise without looking up at the ceiling.

How to do it

❏ Sit down on a chair with feet and knees comfortably spaced apart and hands resting palms down on your thighs just above the knees.
❏ Look up at the ceiling and note what point on it you can see. Don't force your head back or tilt your body backwards: stay within a comfortable range of movement and keep the upper body vertical.
❏ Look straight ahead again. With softly flexed elbow and wrist joints, slowly raise one arm up from your knee to head height and then down again, making a graceful, flowing movement with your hand as though gently stroking the air in front of you. Do this five times.

❏ Do five more repetitions, but this time, as your hand moves upwards, slowly and simultaneously raise the heel of your foot on the same side, keeping your toe in contact with the floor.
❏ Repeat the same sequence with the other hand and then with the other hand and foot.
❏ When you have finished, look up at the ceiling again; you should find that your range of movement has increased, and that you can see a spot further back than you could before.

DO: make your movements slow and fluid.

AVOID: looking downwards as your hand moves downwards, or holding your breath; keep your breathing slow and rhythmic in time with the movement of your arm.

Whip changes

Done correctly this exercise helps improve your general coordination and dexterity and reduces one-sidedness.

Benefits

Changing your whip from one hand to the other correctly is a basic skill which takes only a little practice to master. Improving your ability to do so will not only benefit your horse, but will help improve your general coordination and reduce one-sidedness as well as the inclination to be heavier on the rein with one hand than the other. Some disturbance is inevitable, but excessive clumsiness and fumbling with a whip interferes with the rein contact considerably and can startle the horse, or result in accidentally hitting him. Practise while dismounted until your movements are smooth and easy, and then try again while doing the Bridle exchange exercise with a friend for some first-hand feedback. Finally do the exercise while mounted.

How to do it

To change a short jumping/hacking-type whip from the left hand to the right:
- ❏ place both the reins into the left hand with the whip
- ❏ take hold of the top of the whip with your right hand, placing it above the left one and keeping the thumb uppermost
- ❏ slide the whip up and out of the left hand, bring it across to the right-hand side and take both reins back in both hands again. To change the whip from right to left hand again, simply reverse these instructions.

To change a long dressage whip from the left hand to the right:
- ❏ place both the reins into the left hand with the whip
- ❏ turn your left hand over so that the whip begins to describe an upwards arc in front of you
- ❏ take hold of the whip with your right hand, placing your right thumb next to left little finger, and release it with your left hand
- ❏ continue to swing the whip through an arc in front of you until it is on the right-hand side, and take both reins back in both hands again. To change the whip from the right back to the left hand again, simply reverse these instructions.

DO: choose your moment when changing the whip over while riding – do it before or after a movement, not in the middle of it.

AVOID: looking down at what you're doing, and look straight ahead.

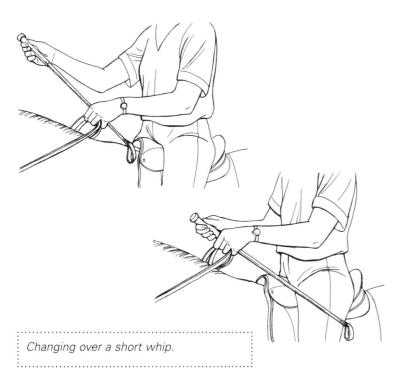

Changing over a short whip.

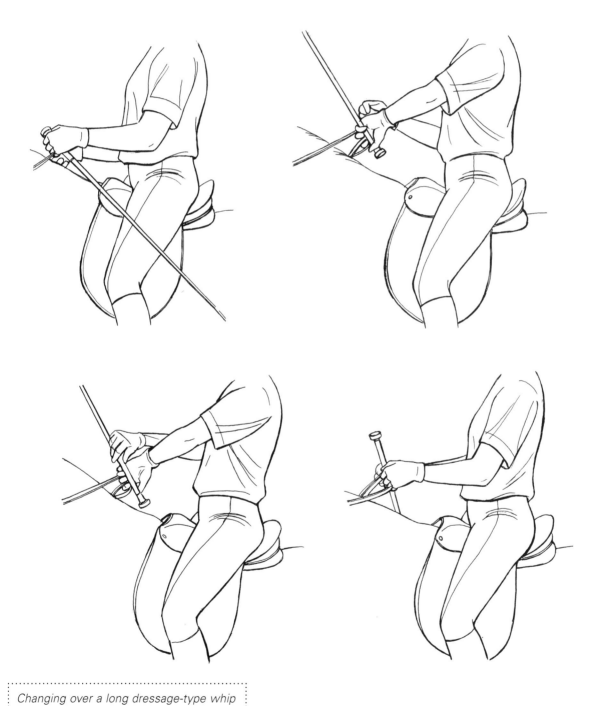

Changing over a long dressage-type whip

Stroking the reins

This exercise helps the rider to relax in his shoulders and lower back and his fingers to be soft on the reins.

Benefits

This is a Connected Riding exercise that benefits both horse and rider. It helps the rider's shoulders and lower back to be relaxed, with the fingers soft rather than clamped on the reins. At the same time the horse learns to release tension and soften through the jaw, poll, neck and back. Try it while doing Exercise 73 Bridle exchange as well as when mounted, so you can appreciate the feel which is created on the receiving end as well.

How to do it

❑ Ask someone to hold your horse in halt – preferably with a lead rein attached to the bridle noseband rather than the bit, so that it doesn't interfere with the connection you are making with the horse's mouth.

❑ Stroke along the reins with a combing action, sliding each hand in turn from just behind the horse's neck to a point just in front of your body.

❑ As one hand begins moving towards you, place the other just ahead of it and begin the next stroking action so that it becomes a continuous soft, rhythmical flow of movement. Keeping your fingers and wrists relaxed will allow your hands to slide along the reins easily.

❑ Try the same exercise in walk, again with someone leading you.

DO: use reins without grips so your fingers slide freely.

AVOID: inadvertently clamping your lower legs on the horse's sides while you are doing this exercise.

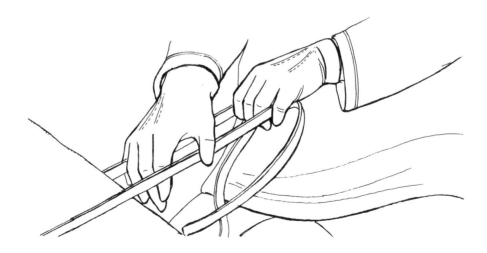

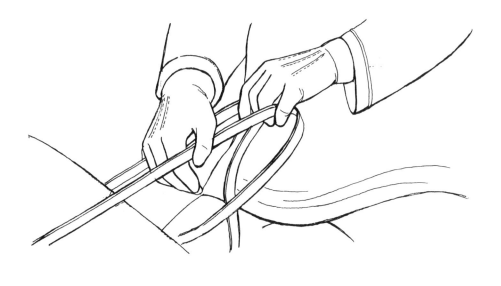

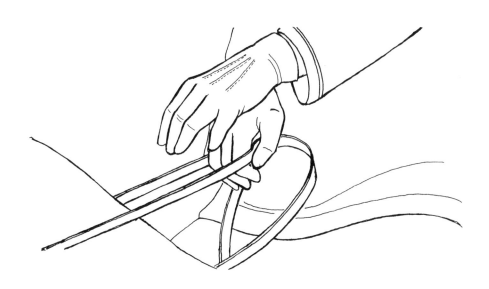

17

DISMOUNTED EXERCISES

'No hour is wasted that is spent in the saddle.'

Winston Churchill 1874–1965: British politician, statesman, soldier, artist, historian

THE EXERCISES

While other sportsmen and women recognize the value of warming up, riders are surprisingly lax about this, even though they appreciate the importance of it for their horses. Doing a few dismounted exercises before riding means that the rider is in a better position to help the horse from the moment he sets foot in the stirrup.

Dismounted exercises can help develop suppleness and flexibility, improve balance and coordination, and increase body awareness as well as the ability to move the limbs independently. If you are unable to ride as frequently as you would like, they can be an invaluable way of working on problem areas and continuing to progress between riding sessions.

This chapter contains a selection of exercises that riders may find helpful, and is by no means an exhaustive list. If you wish to expand your repertoire there are many books and exercise DVDs, amongst other resources, to which you can refer, or you could consult a sports medicine specialist, physiotherapist or fitness trainer for advice.

OTHER EXERCISES

As well as the dismounted exercises suggested in other chapters, some of the mounted ones can also be done while dismounted; for example:

Chapter 5: The head and neck
❏ Exercise 5 Head roll
❏ Exercise 7 Infinity and beyond
❏ Exercise 8 Chin tuck
❏ Exercise 9 Head stretch

Chapter 6: The upper body
❏ Exercise 14 Helicopter

Chapter 7: The shoulders
❏ Exercise 19 Shoulder shrug
❏ Exercise 21 Elbow push
❏ Exercise 22 Arm circling
❏ Exercise 23 Elbow circling

Chapter 8: The arms and wrists
❏ Exercise 25 Arm shake
❏ Exercise 26 Heavy elbows
❏ Exercise 27 Elbow lifts and slides

Chapter 9: The hands
❏ Exercise 30 Finger wiggle

Chapter 11: The feet and ankles
❏ Exercise 43 Ankle circling

How to warm up

Always warm up before doing any exercises, both to maximize their benefit and to avoid risk of injury – warm muscles stretch, but cold ones don't. A brisk 10–15-minute walk should be sufficient, increasing the blood supply to the muscles and helping you to relax. Start off steadily and gradually increase the intensity of the activity until you are really marching along and swinging your arms.

BENEFITS

Studies suggest that as little as a single 15–30-second stretch for each muscle group per day can result in an appreciable increase in the range of movement your body achieves.

Don't overdo it!

When performing stretching exercises, don't overdo things. Stretch as far as feeling a slight pull, but not to the point where you feel sharp pain or intense discomfort, with 30 seconds appearing to be the optimal time to hold a stretch. Breathe in as you begin a stretch and out as you finish it. Do the stretches slowly and gently rather than pushing or bouncing energetically into them. This not only makes them safer to do, but helps increase your coordination and proprioception. Some of the exercises are more challenging than others; don't struggle if you find you can't cope with certain ones, but try an easier substitute instead which will have a similar effect.

EXERCISE

77

Inchworm

Use this exercise to relieve tension in the shoulders.

Benefits

This is a wonderfully relaxing TTouch exercise to do before you mount. It's very good at getting rid of tension in the shoulders and helps them to lower and stretch open rather than round and slump. If your shoulders ache, it's also far more effective than kneading them with your fingers. You can, if necessary, do it on your own, using one hand on the opposite shoulder and then changing over, but better still take it in turns with a friend to help each other as described here.

How to do it

❏ Standing behind your friend, place both hands on their shoulders, one at either side of the base of the neck. Keep your thumbs on the side nearest to you, and fingers facing away.

❏ Using just the weight of your hands, move each hand slowly and steadily towards the other, moving the skin with them, sliding it across the underlying muscle. Only move the hands as far as you can easily move the skin.

❏ Hold for 4 seconds and then slowly move both hands back to and slightly beyond their starting point, again moving the skin with them.

❏ Slowly release the tension, slide the hands slightly further apart from each other and repeat the sequence again. Continue to do this until you have covered the whole of the top of the shoulder area, and then continue down the upper arms to the elbows.

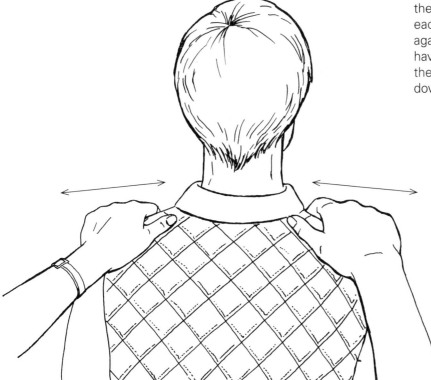

Arm swing

This exercise will increase the range of movement in your upper body and can also be an exercise in coordination.

Benefits
This variation of a Feldenkrais exercise will increase the range of movement in your upper body and help release tension in the neck, back and shoulders.

How to do it
❏ Stand with your feet shoulder width apart and the weight evenly distributed across them.
❏ Hold your right arm out in front of you at shoulder height with the palm of the hand facing down.
❏ Swing it sideways out to your side, keeping it parallel to the ground. Stretch it as far back as you can comfortably manage and then look along your arm, noting the point where your fingertips are pointing.
❏ Look ahead again and slowly bring the arm back in front of you. Swing it out to the side again, keeping it straight but not stiff and at shoulder height. Repeat this five times, keeping your movements slow and deliberate, breathing regularly and taking care not to force the shoulder back or to rotate your upper body with the arm as it swings backwards.

❏ Slowly swing your right arm five more times, but this time turn your head to look away towards the left each time you swing your right arm out to the side. Face forwards again as your arm moves in front of you. This can be an exercise in coordination too, as many people will instinctively turn their head to face in the same direction as the arm is moving.
❏ Swing your right arm back out as far back as you can comfortably do so and once again look along the length of it, seeing how close to the original mark your fingertips are now. Most people find that their range of movement has increased considerably.
❏ Repeat the entire sequence again, this time swinging the left arm.

DO: keep your feet in the same place.

AVOID: forcing your arm back; you shouldn't feel any tension or pull in your neck, shoulder or back.

Side stretch

This exercise will improve your posture if you slump to one side and will also have a toning and suppling effect on your waist area.

Benefits

If you are inclined to collapse to one side through your waist, this exercise can help make you level, as well as generally toning and increasing suppleness through the waist area. Try to stretch to the same amount on both sides, using a mirror to help you assess this.

How to do it

❏ Stand with your feet shoulder width apart. Place your left hand on your left hip and reach up above your head with the right hand.

❏ Slowly lean slightly to the left side from the waist, letting your right hand swing across towards the left side at the same time. Straighten up again so that your upper body is once again upright, keeping your right hand up in the air. Repeat five times.

❏ Switch over the position of your hands and then repeat again, this time leaning towards the right-hand side. Repeat five times.

AVOID: leaning forwards or allowing your head to push forwards.

EXERCISE

80

Stomach toner

If you collapse through the upper body and tend to slouch, this exercise will help improve your posture as well as the efficiency of your leg aids.

Benefits

This exercise is helpful if you tend to slouch and collapse forwards through your upper body. It also helps you learn how to move each leg independently while maintaining the posture and stability of the upper body. The better the upper body posture is, the easier you will find it to move each foot.

How to do it

❏ Sit evenly over the centre of an exercise ball, with both feet shoulder width apart and placed flat on the floor. Your knees should be in line with your the ankles.

❏ Slowly raise the heel of one foot off the floor until just the toe is resting on it. Then lift the whole foot so that it just comes out of contact with the floor. Hold for a count of five and then slowly place your foot back in contact with the floor again, toe first and then heel. As well as noticing how much you need to use the abdominal muscles as you raise your foot, you'll also find you need to use those at the side to help you in keeping your balance and remaining vertical. Repeat with the other foot.

❏ Repeat five times with each leg.

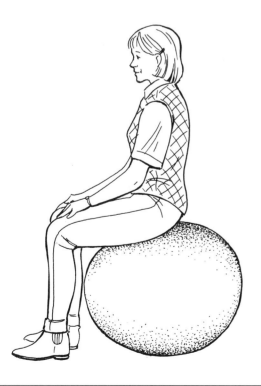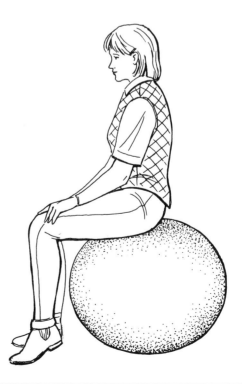

TTouch hand swing

This exercise increases suppleness through the waist while simultaneously improving coordination in your hands and develops the habit of straightness when riding turns and circles.

Benefits

Although this exercise primarily aims to improve suppleness through the waist, it also helps the shoulders to stay open and relaxed. In addition it teaches you how to keep both hands moving smoothly in unison when turning, without collapsing through one side of the waist or leaning into the direction of the hands' movement. This feel will then be easier to duplicate when executing turns and circles while mounted. You will need a second person to partner you.

How to do it

❏ Stand facing each other with your feet positioned comfortably apart and the knees slightly flexed.
❏ The person taking the role of 'horse' crosses one wrist over the other, keeping them lightly touching and with elbows flexed so that the forearms are parallel to the ground.
❏ The 'rider' then lightly links curved fingers with the other person.

❏ The other person then slowly moves their hands to the left, to the middle, and then to the right. The 'rider' shouldn't resist the movement, but should follow it by rotating through the waist and upper body. It may be easier to do this at first with closed eyes.
❏ Try lowering the hands and then raising them too high so you can compare the effects and feel how it interferes with your mobility and coordination.
❏ Take it in turns to swap roles and exchange feedback as to where tension is felt in the 'rider'.

DO: keep both knees equally flexed with your weight equally distributed over both feet – be careful not to let one leg begin to straighten out as your hands move in the opposite direction.

AVOID: leaning to the side as your hands move in that direction; keep both shoulders level.

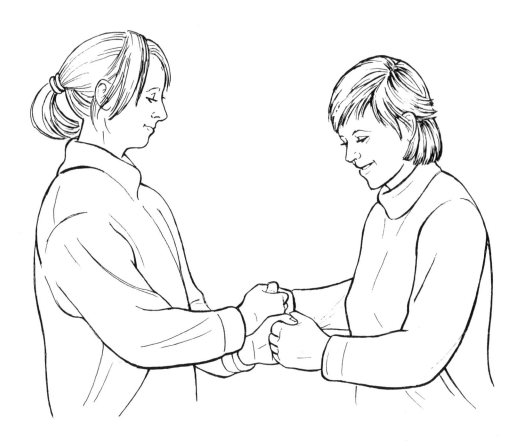

Cat stretch

This exercise is excellent for helping your back muscles to relax and become more flexible and supple.

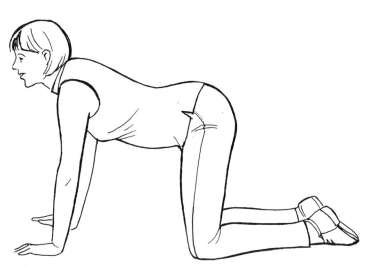

Benefits

This exercise is helpful in creating greater flexibility and suppleness in the back.

How to do it

❏ Get down on to your hands and knees on the floor.
❏ Allow your back to slowly sag downwards – don't forcibly hollow it, just allow yourself to relax completely and let gravity do the rest.
❏ Slowly arch your back upwards away from the floor, like a cat's.

EXERCISE

83

Seat stretcher

This exercise can help you to sit more deeply and securely in the saddle.

Benefits

This exercise rotates the hip joint slightly, helping to open the seat and make it easier for you to sit deeper. The thigh is encouraged to sit flat against the saddle. It also helps if you have a tendency to turn your knees and/or toes outwards when riding, or if you are inclined to grip upwards with the back of your legs.

How to do it

❑ Stand with your feet slightly wider apart than your shoulders, parallel to each other and with your toes facing forwards. Place your hands on the top and front of each thigh.

❑ Try to turn the toes inwards – but without moving your feet. Try also to rotate the whole leg, from the hips, inwards; you should feel your heels pressing more firmly against the ground as you do it, and tension through the front of the thigh. Hold for 30 seconds and then release.

Thigh stretch 1

Your upper body will benefit from this exercise as well as your legs.

Benefits

This exercise helps to stretch the muscle through the front of the thigh, whilst simultaneously encouraging you to lengthen up through the front of the ribcage – but take care not to hollow through your lower back.

How to do it

❏ Place your left hand against a wall or vertical surface, or hold the back of a chair to help balance yourself.

❏ Bring your right foot up behind you and, holding the ankle with your right hand, bring the heel up towards your buttocks pushing the knee backwards until you feel a gentle stretching through the front of the thigh. Hold for 30 seconds and then release.

❏ Repeat with the other leg, using your right hand to support yourself against the wall or chair.

EXERCISE 85

Thigh stretch 2

This exercise is executed lying down, which may be easier for those who find it hard to balance standing up while performing Exercise 84, Thigh stretch 1.

Benefits

If you find it hard to stand on one leg while doing the previous thigh stretch exercise, try this variation instead.

How to do it

❑ Lie down on your left side, stretching out your left arm and supporting your head on it.
❑ Bend your right knee, bringing your right foot up behind you, and hold the ankle with your right hand. Bring the heel up towards your buttocks, and swing the knee backwards until you feel a gentle stretch through the front of the thigh. Hold for 30 seconds and then release.
❑ Roll over on to your right side, and repeat with the other leg.

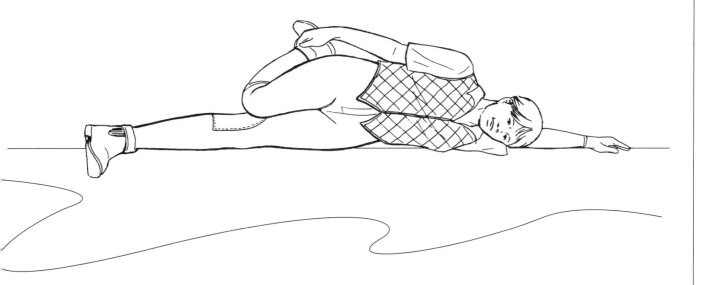

Inner thigh stretch 1

This exercise will help you to ride with a deeper seat and to stretch your legs down around the horse's sides.

Benefits

Stretching the inner thigh muscles will make it easier for you to open and deepen your seat and to stretch the leg down around the horse's sides. Tight inner thigh muscles will squeeze your seat up out of the saddle and will also result in toes and knees turning outwards.

How to do it

❏ Sit upright on the floor and then place the soles of your feet together so they are touching.
❏ Keeping your back straight, lean forwards from the hips towards your feet until you can feel a stretch through the inner thigh. Hold for 30 seconds and relax.

❏ If you find it hard to maintain a good upper body posture, or to bring the soles of the feet together, try sitting on the floor with your legs spread apart in a V shape in front of you. Keeping your back flat, slowly lean forwards, sliding your hands along your legs until you feel a stretch through the inner thigh. Hold for 30 seconds and then relax.

EXERCISE

87

Inner thigh stretch 2

This is another exercise to help you deepen your seat and ride with a more secure leg position.

Benefits
This is an alternative stretching exercise for the inner thigh muscles.

How to do it
- ❏ Stand with your feet comfortably shoulder width apart.
- ❏ Move your weight slightly to the right, flexing your right knee as you do so, and keeping the left leg straight. Be careful not to lean forwards with your upper body. When you feel a gentle stretch in your left leg, hold for 30 seconds, and then relax.
- ❏ Repeat with the right leg.

Hamstring stretch

This exercise can improve your seat and ability to apply effective and accurate lower leg aids.

Benefits

As well as helping you stretch your legs down around the horse, working on this area can also help in drawing your seat bones down into the saddle. It can also improve your ability to apply effective and accurately placed lower leg aids.

How to do it

- ❏ Sit on a chair and place one foot on the seat of another chair or stool.
- ❏ Keeping your back straight, lean slowly forwards towards the raised foot until you feel a stretch; hold for 30 seconds.
- ❏ Repeat with the other foot.

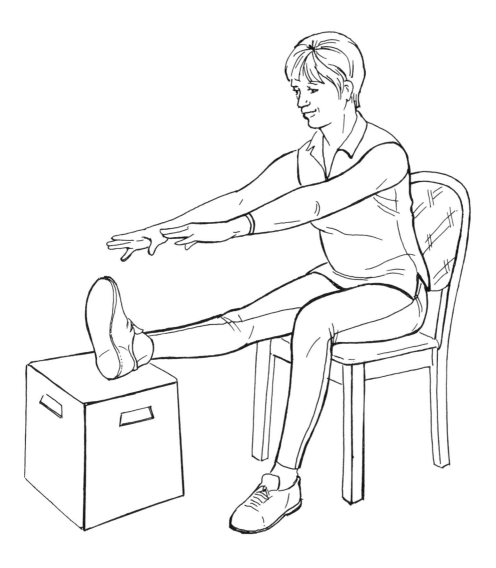

Side leg stretch

This exercise both strengthens weak upper leg muscles and stretches tight ones.

Benefits

This exercise helps improve the range of movement of the hip joint. It also strengthens weak muscles at the top and outside of the thigh and around the hip joint and stretches the inner thigh muscles, which is useful if they are tight.

How to do it

❏ Lie down on your left side and cushion your head with your outstretched arm.
❏ Flex your left knee slightly to help you balance and slowly lift your right leg in the air as high as you can manage. Hold for a count of five, and then slowly lower again.
❏ Repeat five times, then switch sides and repeat with the other leg.

Calf stretch 1

An exercise to help you let the weight down into your heels, creating a more stable lower leg position.

Benefits

This exercise helps stretch the calf muscles so it's easier to let the weight down through your legs into your heels.

How to do it

❑ Stand at arm's length away from a wall, placing the palms of your hands flat against it.
❑ Place your right foot forwards slightly, flexing the knee a little.

❑ Allow your elbows to flex so that you lean forwards towards the wall, keeping the heels of both feet flat on the floor as you do so. Keep your left leg straight.
❑ Hold the stretch for 30 seconds, then return to an upright position again.
❑ Change the position of your legs and repeat the stretch.

EXERCISE

91

Calf stretch 2

This exercise can help stretch tight calf muscles and hamstrings, making it easier for you to let the weight down into your heels.

Benefits
Another calf-stretching exercise; you'll also feel a stretch in the hamstrings at the back of the thighs.

How to do it
❑ Sit on the floor with your legs stretched straight out in front of you.
❑ Keeping your back straight, lean forward and with both hands take hold of the balls of both feet. If it's a struggle to reach, use a folded towel which you can loop around them instead, holding one end of the towel in each hand. Gently apply pressure on the balls of the feet until you feel a stretch in the muscles.
❑ Hold the stretch for 30 seconds.

CHAPTER 18

ONE-SIDEDNESS

'I think it good that the horseman should practise springing up from the off side as well.'

Xenophon 431–353bc, Greek soldier, historian, author

THE EXERCISES

92. Step exercise

93. Pole exercise

94. Sitting

95. Manual dexterity

96. All change

The majority of people are one-sided to some degree, with an estimated 70–90 per cent being right-handed, depending on which studies you consult. Most of the rest are left-handed, although a small number are mixed-handed (where the right hand is favoured for some tasks – for example, writing – and the left hand for others – for example, throwing or catching a ball). Rarer still are those who are truly ambidextrous, able to do things equally well with both hands.

The same bias towards favouring one hand also applies to your legs: if you are right-handed it's quite probable that you are also right-footed, although this isn't always the case. It's possible to be right-handed and left-footed, and vice versa.

The effects of one-sidedness...

... on your hands

The hands take different roles, with the dominant (preferred) one being used for more delicate, precise movements and the non-dominant one for broader, less refined actions. For example, the left hand may hold a needle steady or keep a piece of paper still while the right one threads a piece of cotton through the needle's eye, or writes a few sentences.

... on your legs

If you kick a football you'll favour using one foot over the other, and if you shut your eyes and try to walk a straight line you'll soon end up straying to one side. This of course helps explain why people who are lost in wild areas without any visual references to help guide them often end up walking in a large circle.

... on your riding

Obviously this is all going to have an effect on your riding. One hand may be heavier on one rein than the other, or rein and leg aids on one side may lack the subtlety, accuracy or good timing of their opposites. Certainly most of us are probably familiar with the frustrations when riding of finding that one hand is more inclined to be fixed and rigid, or one leg being less easy to control and keep in the right place. Just as importantly, this natural bias towards one-sidedness influences your ability to be straight in the saddle and further increases the likelihood of either creating or further emphasizing one-sidedness in the horse. Although you are unlikely ever to become completely ambidextrous unless born that way, the closer you can get to that ideal the easier everything will be for both you and your horse.

Step exercise

This exercise will help you make a more equal effort with both legs, so you can control their movement and position with a more similar degree of efficiency and accuracy. It will also improve your balance and straightness, as extreme right or left-leggedness can affect this.

Benefits

This exercise is aimed at encouraging your legs to be a better matched pair. As with your hands, you'll be inclined to favour one more than the other, better able to control its movements and position. At the same time it helps improve your balance, which can be affected considerably by more extreme 'right' or 'left-leggedness'.

How to do it

❏ When climbing stairs it's likely that you will automatically adjust your stride so that your more dominant foot is raised and placed on the first step, while the other leg supports your weight. Slow your approach and consciously adjust your stride so that the less dominant foot is the first one to take up position on the lowest step instead.

❏ Bring the dominant foot up to join the non-dominant one on the same step, then place the dominant foot on the next step and bring the non-dominant one up to join it as before.

❏ Continue up the stairs, taking it in turns to place each foot on the next step and bringing the other one up to join it.

DO: pause for a moment before moving on to each next step, so that you adjust your balance each time and make a more equal effort with both legs.

Moving on

Also practise kicking a ball against a wall with your less dominant foot, fielding it each time with the same foot. This is another good way of improving balance, leg coordination and subtlety of movement in your weaker leg.

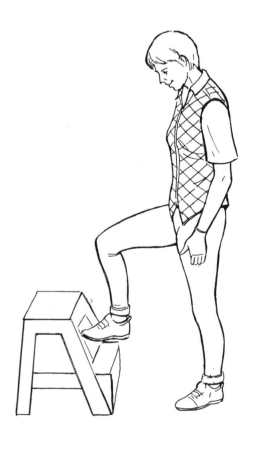

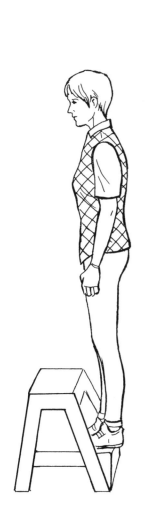

Pole exercise

This TTouch exercise can help you become more level by freeing up the lower back and pelvic region. Doing it slowly will show up incorrect balance and natural bias better, making it easier for you to improve it.

Benefits

Polework isn't just for horses. This TTouch exercise tells you a lot about your stability and coordination, and helps free the lower back and pelvic region as well as encouraging you to be more central in your posture, rather than favouring your more dominant side.

How to do it

❏ Set out a single pole – a jump pole is ideal, but even an old broom handle will do if nothing else is available.
❏ Weave your feet across it, keeping your feet close to each side of the pole. Notice how much arm and upper body movement you use to compensate for tension in the lower back. If this is excessive, try some of the exercises described in other chapters to help reduce this and improve suppleness.

AVOID: stiffening the knee joints, as this will make it harder for you to balance. Also avoid doing this exercise fast to try and compensate for lack of balance. If you keep your movements slow this will show up incorrect balance and natural bias better, and makes it easier to improve it.

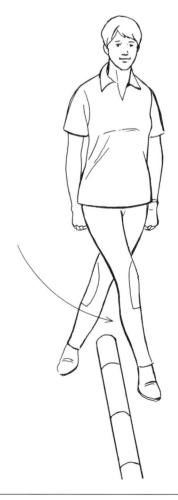

EXERCISE

94

Sitting

This is an exercise in day-to-day deportment because you need to consider and, if necessary, to change how you sit in your daily routine, which may be in a way that predisposes you to one-sidedness and crookedness.

Benefits

Except when in the saddle, the way we sit is something most of us rarely think about, even though we spend a considerable amount of time in a sitting position, and frequently sit very badly from the point of view of posture. This can also contribute to, and reinforce, a tendency to one-sidedness and crookedness, and can be a cause of back problems.

How to do it

❏ If you normally cross your legs, try crossing them so that the leg which is normally on top is underneath. Better still, try to avoid crossing them at all!

❏ When relaxing at home, try not to sit with your legs curled up beneath you as this will increase the tendency to collapse to one side through your waist. If you normally sit at one end of the sofa, sit at the other end, as it's likely you will lean to one side against the arm rest.

❏ If you spend much time at work or at home sitting in front of a computer, make sure you have a suitable chair, adjusted at the right height for your desk. Try to avoid slumping or leaning to one side, and take breaks occasionally to do a few stretching exercises.

Manual dexterity

There are several activities you can fit into your daily routine that will help to even up one-sidedness in your hands. Below are just a few that you might like to try.

Benefits
These exercises are aimed at increasing the dexterity of your non-dominant hand.

How to do it
- ❏ Use your computer mouse with your non-dominant hand.
- ❏ Practise bouncing a tennis ball against the ground or a wall, or play catch with a friend – but catching the ball in your non-dominant hand.
- ❏ Buy a squeezy 'stress ball' and knead it with your less dominant hand.
- ❏ Learn to play a keyboard instrument as this will also improve the suppleness of the fingers.

All change

Often the way we do things in our daily habits serves to reinforce one-sidedness. Here are a few ways in which you can change these habits, thereby improving straightness, posture and, by implication, the way you ride.

Benefits

There are many other things you can do during the course of the day to help decrease the discrepancy between the right- and left-hand sides; one-sidedness is often reinforced by habit, and this carries through into your riding. By changing some of those daily habits and increasing your adroitness, coordination and body awareness, you'll make it easier to shed bad riding habits and make new postural corrections, as well as improving straightness in your riding and communication with your horse.

How to do it

- ❏ Change over your knife and fork and use them in the opposite hands from what is usual for you.
- ❏ Pick up the phone with your non-dominant hand.
- ❏ Use the TV remote control with your non-dominant hand.
- ❏ Put your shoulder bag over the opposite shoulder from normal, or carry your briefcase in the other hand.
- ❏ When dressing, you'll probably always put the same foot first into the leg of your trousers and the same arm first into the sleeve of your top or jacket; do it the other way round instead.
- ❏ Lift your glass or coffee mug with your non-dominant hand.

- ❏ When sweeping the yard, swap over your hands on the broom handle, so that the hand which is normally higher is lower, and the broom is on your other side. Do the same when doing household chores. For example, do the dusting and push the vacuum cleaner with the non-dominant hand.
- ❏ Brush your hair holding the brush in your non-dominant hand.

STRAIGHTNESS

'Every rider who guides his horse well in straight lines will also guide him well in corners.'

Gaspard de Saunier 1663–1748: French soldier, equestrian and author on classical horsemanship

THE EXERCISES

It is often said that a crooked rider can never straighten a crooked horse. Equally, a crooked rider will soon make a straight horse crooked. Sitting crookedly affects rider balance, security, suppleness and coordination, and since it affects the horse's ability to move straight, will impede impulsion and free forward movement as well as creating conflict and resistance when you ask him to do something. Crookedness can also place strain on the back and limb joints of both horse and rider, leading to injury.

TIP

Read Chapter 18 in conjunction with this one, because one-sidedness can influence straightness.

Getting yourself straight in the saddle

Sitting straight isn't always easy and is even harder when riding a horse that is markedly crooked itself. Like us, equines are also inclined to one-sidedness, but it is absolutely vital that we sit straight if we are to influence, rather than be influenced by, the horse. Getting (and keeping) yourself straight in the saddle can be one of the most challenging problems to sort out, and the help of someone else who can watch and tell you whether you are straight is a real asset because it can be notoriously difficult to determine this yourself, given the body's ability to deceive itself that all is well.

It's worth persevering!

If you are accustomed to sitting crookedly, it can feel quite awkward, even uncomfortable, when you do sit straight. As the benefits can sometimes take time to become apparent, it can be hard to feel motivated to keep putting effort into it. Yet it will pay off handsomely if you do, in that your horse will be more willing and better able to work without resistance on either rein and will do so more comfortably and smoothly, with better balance, poise and impulsion and with increased responsiveness to your aids.

Asymmetry is 'normal'

Everyone is asymmetric to some degree – our internal organs aren't symmetrically arranged and externally, neither is each half of our body an exact mirror image of the opposite side. It is not uncommon to have one leg longer than the other, and in instances where there is a very marked discrepancy in length between the two, it may be necessary for you to ride with one stirrup a little longer than the other in order to keep your spine straight and remain level in the saddle.

Investigate any problems

For most of us the difference is, however, very minimal and our musculature compensates successfully enough that we are unaware of it. However, should you suspect that any aches and pains you experience, or difficulty in sitting straight, stem from this, consult a sports physiotherapist or similar expert who can take proper and accurate measurements and decide on the best way of resolving the problem. Simply deciding you have one leg longer than the other without any proper investigation, and adjusting your stirrups accordingly, can end up creating more problems, distortions and discomfort than you started with.

The effects of centrifugal force

When working through turns and circles, centrifugal force will have an effect on the rider's straightness, causing the seat to slip towards the outside. The smaller the radius of the circle or turn, and the greater the gait speed, the more pronounced centrifugal force becomes.

In order to remain straight, the rider needs to think about stabilizing himself by stretching through the inside of the waist, whil simultaneously stretching down through the inside leg. This will also have the effect of subtly increasing the pressure of the rider's inside seatbone on the saddle, which in turn encourages the horse to step more actively beneath himself with his inside hind leg. This also helps him to be more perpendicular to the ground and less likely to lean inwards and 'motorbike' through turns and circles.

On the lunge

❏ When the rider is being lunged and therefore circling constantly, it can increase the likelihood of crookedness creeping in unless a watchful eye is kept for telltale signs that the rider is slipping to the side (see Troubleshooting, p. 214).

❏ The rein should be changed several times during a lesson so that both pupil and horse work equally on both sides; on each occasion the teacher should take the opportunity to check on rider straightness from in front before recommencing work on the new rein.

❏ Care must be taken not to make the circle too small – this will put an increased strain on the horse, as well as making it more difficult for the rider to stay straight.

TIP

When riding out with a friend, take it in turns to ride behind each other so you can observe and help each other with straightness. Avoid wearing stripy shirts – both horizontal and vertical stripes can mislead the eye as to what the shoulders and torso are really doing.

Hands out

This exercise encourages riders who tend to keep looking down to look up and in front of them, as well as helping improve straightness.

Benefits

This exercise can be performed on the lunge or while being led, and helps develop balance as well as straightness. It also encourages those riders who are in the habit of looking down, to look up and ahead.

How to do it

❏ Raise both arms to shoulder height in front of you, moving them slowly so as not to startle the horse. Keep your hands spaced at shoulder width apart, palms facing towards each other.

❏ Both hands should be at the same height – if you are leaning or slipping to one side it quickly becomes obvious, because the hands will no longer be opposite each other. At the same time, you will become more aware of keeping your weight evenly distributed across your seat, and of letting the legs drop down from your hips on each side of the horse.

❏ Should you start to lose balance, hold the mane or neckstrap while the horse halts, and then centre yourself once more and try again.

DO: try this exercise in walk to start with, only progressing to sitting trot when you feel confident, balanced and straight.

AVOID: curling your fingers into fists – if you do, it is probably because you are beginning to lose balance.

Straightness is as important when jumping as when riding on the flat.

Centring the seat

This exercise is a check you can make each time you halt or give your horse a rest.

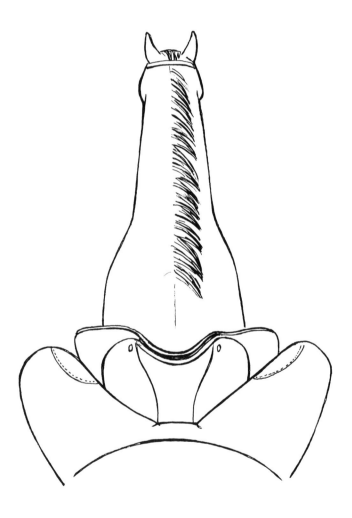

Benefits

Every time you mount, spend a moment or two before you move off trying to get your weight as equally distributed across the saddle as possible. Check again each time you halt or give your horse a breather. This exercise can be combined with Exercise 44 Toe straightener.

How to do it

❏ Ask your horse to stand squarely. If he's resting a leg or leaving one behind him, his back won't be level, and neither will you be when you then move off!

❏ Glance down and check that the centre seam on your jodhpurs is aligned with the centre of the saddle's pommel.

❏ Align your breastbone with the seam and pommel too, so that it is directly above the horse's spine.

❏ Look at your knees, which should both appear to be the same height, not one higher or further forward than the other.

❏ If your seat is a little to one side, place the reins in one hand and with the other hand on the front of the saddle, gently shift your seat across until you judge that you are as central as you can possibly make yourself.

❏ If available, use mirrors as well to check on yourself, or ask anyone else who may be around to take a look.

DO: remember to look up and ahead again, once you have glanced down to check on your position.

THE 'SPINAL TWIST'

The old advice of keeping your hips parallel to the horse's hips and your shoulders parallel with the horse's shoulders still tends to persist, but attempting to twist in this way will put your back under strain and will inevitably cause crookedness. Keep your shoulders parallel to your own hips and both so they are at right angles across the horse's spine.

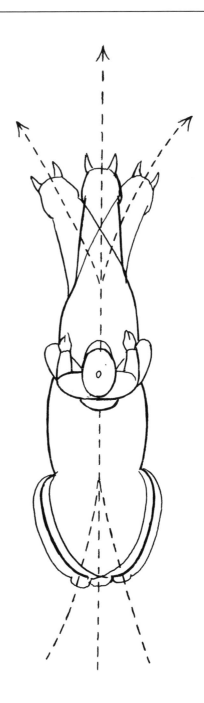

Glider

This exercise encourages the rider to lower and relax the shoulders and to open the front of the chest, as well as increasing awareness of straightness and balance.

Benefits

Another exercise to perform on the lunge or while being led, which helps improve straightness and balance. It also encourages the shoulders to lower and relax and the front of the chest to open, with the rider stretching up through the front of the ribcage.

How to do it

❏ Raise both arms up to shoulder height at both sides. Keep the palms of your hands uppermost and raise your arms slowly so you don't startle the horse.

❏ Both arms should be at the same height. Any tilting due to your seat slipping to one side or collapsing through one side of your waist is easy for an onlooker to spot, although you may be less aware of it unless it's extreme. It does, however, increase your awareness of the position of your seat in the saddle. It also uses both the abdominal muscles at the front and the oblique muscles at the side of your torso to greater effect to keep your upper body vertical and straight.

❏ If you start to lose your balance, use the mane or neckstrap to help you rebalance. Halt, centre yourself again and try once more.

DO: try the exercise at walk first, progressing to sitting to the trot when you feel balanced and confident.

AVOID: making your arms rigid, but keep a slight flexion in the elbows and allow the fingers to be soft and slightly curved.

Hand on back

If you turn the shoulders too much to the inside when you are riding turns or circles, this exercise will help.

Benefits

This exercise will help if you are inclined to draw your outside shoulder back.
It can also be used to correct a tendency to overturn the shoulders to the inside through turns and circles. It can be done while being led or lunged and also while riding independently, provided you can control your horse while riding with the reins in one hand.

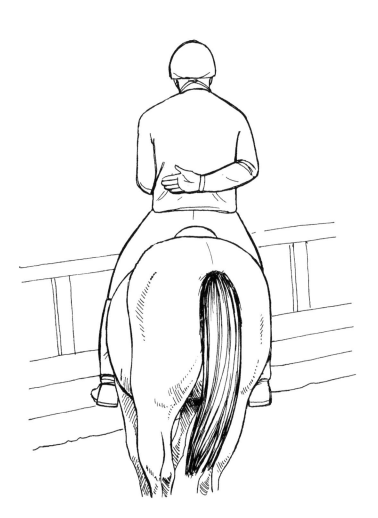

How to do it

❏ Hold both the reins in your outside hand. Place your inside arm behind your back so the forearm is parallel to the ground. Keep your hand open and your palm facing outwards away from your body.

❏ Gently stretch across with your fingertips towards your waist on the opposite side. This will encourage you to sit in harmony with the horse through turns and circles, keeping your shoulders and hips square across the horse's spine rather than drawing the outside shoulder back and pushing the inside one forwards.

❏ If you have the opposite problem and tend to overturn your shoulders towards the inside, place the reins in your inside hand instead and the outside hand behind your back. This can be helpful where centrifugal force is causing the problem, because it will make it easier for you to keep your seat straight in the saddle as well as to stretch through the inside of your waist and through the inside leg.

AVOID: allowing yourself to lean inwards over the arm which is behind your back. Endeavour to keep your shoulders level, as this will help.

101

Waist stretch

By encouraging the rider to stretch through the side of their waist, this exercise helps those who tend to collapse to one side in that area.

Benefits

Exercise 13 Hands in the air is excellent for preventing a tendency to collapse through one side of your waist, but because it's not always practical to ride around with the reins in one hand and the other hand up in the air, you'll need to employ some visualization and increase your body awareness.

How to do it

❑ Do Exercise 13 to help produce an upright and straight posture through your ribcage.
❑ Concentrate on how it feels, then help yourself to maintain it by thinking about stretching the side of your waist through which you tend to collapse.
❑ At the same time stretch downwards through the leg on that side. Allow the thigh to drop down away from your hip rather than pushing your heel deeper, because doing so will push your seat to the opposite side and will result in collapsing again.

AVOID: raising your shoulder when stretching through the side of your waist.

TROUBLESHOOTING

This index relates to specific problems that are discussed in the following Troubleshooting section.

In this section you will find all the common problems that riders face, handily arranged by area of the body, so that they correspond to the exercise chapters. The fault or problem is identified and its cause explained, with references given to exercises that will help you to resolve the problem.

If you find a problem in the following pages that relates to your riding then follow the page references to the relevant chapter for a range of exercises that can help you.

Chapter 9: The hands
Very low hands
Unlevel hands
One hand higher than the other
Holding the reins too tightly
Pushing/pulling with the hands
Hands turned over
Hands pulling backwards
Hands rising up and down
Hands curved round in front of
  the rider
Hands too far apart

Chapter 10: The legs
Legs swinging back too far
Legs swinging backwards when
  jumping
Lower legs too far forwards
One leg swinging forwards and out
  of contact

Legs shooting outwards during the
  rising phase of rising to the trot
Gripping with knees and thighs
Legs turning outwards from hips

Chapter 11: The feet and ankles
Toes turn outwards
Toes down/heels up
Gripping up with the heels
Heels too deep
Too much weight on the outside of
  the stirrup
Losing stirrups

Chapter 19: Straightness
Losing the inside stirrup/gripping up
  with the inside leg
Outside lower leg swinging
  forwards
Looking down to one side
Leaning to one side
One hand higher than the other
One shoulder higher than the other
Off-centre jodhpur seam
Feeling of slipping to one side
One knee or foot higher than the
  other
Outside shoulder moving too far
  forwards/the inside shoulder
  moving too far back

THE SEAT

Fork seat If the rider's seat is tilting forwards on to the crotch, it will cause the upper body to tip forwards. If an effort is then made to bring the upper body into a vertical position without first correcting the seat, it will cause hollowing, and consequently stiffening, through the back. A fork seat may also cause the legs to swing too far back, the heels to rise and the thighs and knees to grip inwards; the rider is likely to be in front of the movement and may be inclined to rest the hands on the horse's neck for support. The same effect can be produced if the stirrup leathers are too long, or if the rider has been told to 'sit taller' and straighter without being shown how to do it properly, without pushing the chest forwards excessively or hollowing the back.

Chair seat Sitting, literally, as though in a chair is likely to lead to the lower leg being pushed too far forwards and the heel too deep, locking the ankle, knee and hip joints. The upper body is liable to slump and the shoulders to round, with the rider being behind the movement and probably using the reins for support. This can also occur as a result of a rider constantly being encouraged to 'tuck his tail' under him instead of being properly shown how to find the right position for his seat.

Sitting crookedly If the rider's weight is unevenly distributed across the saddle it will unbalance the horse as well as the rider and is likely to give rise to further postural problems, as well as back ache for both; this aspect is covered in Chapter 18, One-sidedness and Chapter 19, Straightness.

For exercises that will help with your seat see Chapter 4, The seat, pp. 30–33.

Correct seat

Fork seat

Chair seat

THE HEAD AND NECK

Looking down This is a very common fault in many riders. If lacking 'feel' it is tempting to look down to check canter leads, trotting diagonals, bend, and generally to try and see what the horse is doing – in spite of the fact that you can see very little of it while mounted. It can lead to rounded shoulders, collapsing through the torso and inaccurate riding. It is a potentially dangerous fault, not just because it can affect security and balance in the saddle, but because it reduces rider awareness of surroundings and the possible hazards which may be lurking in them.

Nodding head This is most often seen when the rider is in sitting trot, usually as a way of compensating for stiffness in the lower back and hips. Rather than absorbing the horse's movement in the right places, the head, sometimes accompanied by the shoulders, tends to nod and wobble. The torso may also be collapsed and behind the movement, and a 'chair' seat could be at the root of the problem.

Head tilted to one side Head tilting may occur in particular when riding turns and circles, during lateral work, or if the rider is sitting crookedly. It can also be just a postural habit, or it may happen when listening to comments from a teacher, or to a friend who is chatting while riding out, or to the rhythm and tempo of the horse's hooves. Left uncorrected it will lead to, or further accentuate, any crookedness present and also to inaccurate riding of school figures.

Jutting chin This characteristic may be accompanied by tight jaw muscles and clenched teeth. It can be due to apprehension, irritation, intense concentration or even determination to succeed at a task perceived as being difficult. This tension will spread to the neck and shoulders, causing stiffness and possible hollowing through the back.

For exercises that will help with your head and neck see Chapter 5, The head and neck, pp. 34–41.

THE UPPER BODY

'Belly-dancing' tummy This is usually most apparent in sitting trot and is often accompanied by a nodding head. Trying to absorb the horse's movement in this way creates an unstable posture, interferes with the ability to sit deep and also creates difficulty with the application of the leg, seat and back aids. A chair seat, stiffness in the hip area, rounded shoulders, looking down and collapsing through the ribcage can all contribute to the problem.

Bouncing in the saddle Bouncing may be due to:
❏ gripping with the knees and thighs
❏ the stirrups being excessively short
❏ stiffness in the back and hips
❏ being behind the movement
❏ locking through the hip, knee and ankle joints
❏ holding your breath.

Rocking the upper body Stiffness in the lower back may lead to the upper body rocking back and forth in an attempt to absorb the movement instead; it is often especially noticeable in canter.

It is also frequently due to the rider endeavouring to get a lazy horse going forwards more actively; such animals can encourage tense posture and an exaggerated backwards-forwards pushing with the seat and upper body. A feeling of opening the hips and allowing the legs to stretch down will help to resolve the problem and enable the rider to apply more effective leg aids.

Collapsing the upper body Usually accompanied and accentuated by rounded shoulders and a tendency to look downwards. A curved 'banana' shape may be due to a chair seat, or to the rider trying to make himself softer and more supple, or to the reins being too long; it may also be a habitual posture. Tall riders may often round the shoulders and stoop through the ribcage because of self-consciousness about their height, and this inhibited feeling can carry through to when they are riding.

Hollowed back Hollowing the back makes the rider very stiff and unable to absorb the horse's movement correctly; it also tends to lock the hips, making it hard to apply effective leg aids. It may be due to a fork seat, to the stirrups being too long because the chest has been pushed forwards too much, or to the rider trying to sit taller without being shown how to do so correctly.

Tipping forwards This places the rider in front of the movement, making him unbalanced, insecure and likely to rest his hands on the horse's neck for support. It may be due to the stirrups being too long, a fork seat, and/or hollowing the back. When sitting with the upper body vertical, the rider may feel initially as though he is leaning backwards.

Leaning backwards This problem may be due to the reins being too long, because the rider is trying to force the seat down into the saddle instead of correctly absorbing the movement, or he is trying to drive the horse forwards.

The latter tends to be a very aggressive action, which is likely to cause the horse to run forwards and to hollow its back. Riders who are in the habit of riding with the upper body behind the vertical may actually feel as though they are tipping forwards when they are sitting correctly.

Collapsing through one side of the waist Generally this fault occurs because the seat has slipped to one side and is no longer central. The upper body tries to compensate by leaning inwards in the opposite direction. It can also occur if the stirrups are unlevel, during turns and circles, and can be a habitual postural habit – see also Chapter 18 One-sidedness and Chapter 19 Straightness for exercises to help.

For exercises that will help with your upper body see Chapter 6, The upper body, pp. 42–57.

THE SHOULDERS

Although normally the shoulders should be aligned directly above the hip bones when viewed in profile, there are occasions when this rule of thumb doesn't apply – for example when jumping, galloping, rising to the trot, or when going up or down gradients; see also Chapter 6, The upper body. However, whatever the activity, both shoulders should constantly remain level with each other and an equal distance from each hip bone.

One shoulder higher than the other This fault is often due to crookedness, which can have a number of causes; most commonly it stems from the seat slipping to one side and collapsing through one side of the waist. The saddle should also be checked for correct fitting. The shoulder is higher on the side the seat is slipping and lower on the opposite side, on which the waist is collapsed. Crookedness, and its causes and remedies, is discussed in greater detail in Chapter 19, Straightness.

Raised shoulders If both shoulders are raised this may be due to stiffness, or to lack of balance – for example the rider is attempting to use them to help lift the seat out of the saddle in rising trot.

This can also occur when the rider makes an incorrect effort to sit up taller.

Tight, tense shoulders Tension across the shoulders can be due to general stiffness in the area, but apprehension or stress can also be responsible. Jutting the chin forwards can also lead to tension in the shoulders.

Round shouldered Very often this posture accompanies a collapsed ribcage, which can be a consequence of lazy posture, a chair seat, the lower leg being too far forward, or the reins too long. It may also be due to the shoulders attempting to absorb the horse's movement, rather than the seat, legs and lower back. Looking downwards also encourages round shoulders. Sometimes it is the rider's natural shape, in which case you may not be able to change it a great deal, although things may be improved a little. Indeed, developing a correct, upright posture while on a horse can lead to postural improvements in a more general sense for the individual concerned.

For exercises that will help with your shoulders see Chapter 7, The shoulders, pp. 58–69.

THE ARMS AND WRISTS

Elbows clamped to the sides This fault may either be the cause of, or the result of, tight, raised shoulders. Working on this area, too, will be beneficial. It can also be as a result of over-compensating for sticking out elbows.

Elbows sticking out There may be several reasons why a rider's elbows stick out:
- ❏ the reins are too long
- ❏ the hands are turned over so the backs are facing upwards instead of outwards
- ❏ the wrists are over-curved
- ❏ the rider's shoulders are raised and stiff.

'Flyaway' elbows can often give the rider the feeling of being very independent and flexible through the arm, but in fact they cause the hands to draw back and the reins to be used for support. When jumping the same set of reasons may cause flyaway elbows, but they can also result from a lack of rider confidence, or because the rider 'picks the horse up' with the reins on take-off, or stands up in the stirrups instead of folding the upper body forwards.

Elbows drawing back behind the ribcage When this happens it is usually due to excessively long reins; it is often accompanied by the upper body tipping forwards.

Stiff, rigid arms This may be a result of the rider trying to force himself into a correct position and is usually linked to general stiffness with lack of suppleness through the whole body.

Lack of flexion in the elbows If the elbows are not flexed sufficiently the reins may be too short. If the hands are carried very low (usually because of tipping forwards and for support) this can also lead to the arms becoming straight, stiff and lacking flexion at the elbows.

Rounded wrists Rounding the wrists often accompanies rounded shoulders and a tendency to collapse through the ribcage. It can also happen when the reins are slightly too long.

Hollowed wrists If the wrists are hollowed, as opposed to being rounded, check that the shoulders aren't also hunched and tight. Exercises to help the shoulders and encourage relaxed elbow joints may be of help, as well as those for the wrists themselves.

For exercises that will help with your arms and wrists see Chapter 8, The arms and wrists, pp. 70–79.

THE HANDS

Very low hands Low hands encourage the horse to resist and become fixed through the neck and jaw, as well as to lean forwards on to the forehand. This hand position is frequently due to the rider tipping forwards and using the reins for support. Check general posture, trying to become more upright through the torso and checking that the elbows are flexed with the hands carried clear of the horse's withers. Oddly enough, the opposite of this problem is uncommon – you rarely see a rider carrying their hands too high.

Unlevel hands One hand drawing further back than the other may be due to one rein being longer than the other, or to the rider sitting crookedly with one shoulder drawing backwards. Incorrectly applied rein aids can also be responsible – for example pulling the inside hand backwards to ride a turn or circle.

One hand higher than the other If one hand is held higher than the other, this can lead to the horse tilting his head, as well as an increased upward feel on one side of the horse's mouth, which may create discomfort and bit evasions. There may be occasions when raising one or even both hands is appropriate, but such rein actions should be carried out with delicacy and control and with definite conscious intent and full understanding of what you are trying to achieve, rather than being due to poor posture. This may occur for a variety of reasons: one rein being longer than the other, sitting crookedly, leaning inwards, or collapsing through one side of the waist.

Holding the reins too tightly This fault may be due to tension and anxiety. It is often linked to tension in the jaw, too.

Pushing/pulling with the hands This action is often accompanied by a backward and forward rocking of the upper body. Tipping forwards causes the knee and thigh to tighten, making the leg aids less effective as well as disturbing horse and rider balance, and gives rise to pushing and pulling with the hands and torso in an attempt to generate some impulsion.

Hands turned over This hand position is often described as 'playing the piano' and can be due to the elbows sticking out.

Hands pulling backwards Hands that pull backwards may be the result of reins that are too long, lack of balance, or lack of suppleness. When jumping, this can also be due to the rider attempting to 'pick the horse up' on take-off, or due to their standing up in the stirrups instead of folding, or of being left behind and failing to let the reins slide through the fingers. If the hands have a tendency to pull backwards and become restrictive on the approach to a fence, it can also be due to lack of rider confidence.

Hands rising up and down This often happens in canter, also in rising trot when the hands move up and down with the rider. It is usually due to lack of suppleness and balance through the rest of the body; it may also be due to excessively energetic leg aids.

Hands curved round in front of the rider This position is caused by over-rounding of the wrists; it may feel as though you are being soft and flexible, but holding the hands like this creates a restrictive contact that blocks the free forward movement of the horse.

Hands too far apart If you are holding your hands too far apart it is usually because your reins are too long. Although it may be necessary to have the hands slightly wider apart than the ideal when riding young, very green horses through turns and circles, beware of it becoming a habit. Carrying the hands too far apart will make it more difficult to have a sympathetic and consistent contact, the horse's shoulders will be inclined to drift and it is harder to keep both hands the same height.

For exercises that will help with your shoulders see Chapter 9, The hands, pp. 80–91.

THE LEGS

Legs swinging too far back Generally due to tipping forwards with the upper body as a result of a fork seat, or because the stirrups are too long.

Legs swinging backwards when jumping Usually due to insufficient weight being put into the heels, leading to lack of stability in the lower leg. It may also occur if the stirrups are too long, or the rider stands up in the stirrups on take-off instead of folding forwards. This can make it hard to recover on the landing side of the fence, unbalancing the horse. Exercises to supple the ankles and stretch the calf muscles may help, plus practising the jumping position while dismounted.

Lower legs too far forwards May be due to tight hip and thigh muscles, making it hard to stretch the leg downwards beneath the seat. The stirrups may also be too short, or the rider may be pushing the heels down too deeply.

One leg swinging forwards and out of contact This may arise due to crookedness, if the rider is twisting through the upper body, or if the seat slips to one side. The waist may be collapsed on the opposite side to the leg which is swinging forwards and out of contact.

Legs shooting outwards during the rising phase of rising trot Due to standing up in the stirrups, instead of allowing the horse's back to do the work of pushing the hips and seat forwards and upwards. Exercises 48 Hovering trot and 51 Rising to the trot without stirrups may help.

Gripping with knees and thighs Often linked with tipping forwards and a fork seat.

Legs turning outwards from hips The knees and toes will turn out too, and the buttock muscles may be tight and clenched. Exercise 44 Toe straightener may help.

For exercises that will help with your legs see Chapter 10, The legs, pp. 92–99.

THE FEET AND ANKLES

Toes turn outwards This position can lead to gripping upwards with the back of the legs (the saddle flaps may sometimes be seen bunching up beneath the knees and thighs when this happens) and leg aids will lack subtlety, the legs tending to be either gripping or kicking. The knees may also (not always) point outwards, the buttock muscles will be inclined to be tight and clenched, and there may be difficulty in maintaining a steady lower leg position in rising trot.

Toes down/heels up Such a foot position may occur for a number of reasons, including the stirrups being too long, or the foot having slipped through the iron up to the instep. It can be due to stiff ankle joints and tight calf muscles, as well as from placing the toes on the tread of the irons instead of the balls of the feet so that a tiptoe position is adopted. This can lead to unwanted movement in the lower leg, ineffective, flapping aids and general stiffness with lack of balance in the upper body.

Gripping up with the heels Gripping inwards and upwards may be due to a rider's stirrups being excessively short and/or because they tend to rely on the leg for security. Exercises to improve confidence and balance (see Chapter 12, Balance and Coordination), as well as those that are aimed at helping to stretch and allow weight down through the leg, will be beneficial.

Heels too deep Too much weight in the heel can arise through the over-correction of stiff ankles and tight calf muscles and through the use of angled stirrup irons. Excessively deep heels can cause the ankles, and to a certain extent the knee joints, to become fixed, so they act less efficiently as shock absorbers and in the application of leg aids. The result is that the lower legs are pushed too far forwards.

Too much weight on the outside of the stirrup If too much weight is carried on the outside of the stirrup iron, the lower inner leg will appear to be curled inwards around the horse's sides. This makes it hard to sit deeply and to apply effective aids, possibly causing the knees to sit away from the saddle. Exercises that 'widen' and 'deepen' the seat will help, as will making a conscious effort to spread the weight evenly across the ball of the foot.

Losing stirrups The stirrups may be too long. If one stirrup is lost more frequently than the other, it may be due to rider crookedness or having unlevel stirrups.

For exercises that will help with your shoulders see Chapter 11, The feet and ankles, pp. 100–105.

STRAIGHTNESS

Losing the inside stirrup/gripping up with the inside leg This may be due to the seat slipping towards the outside – as a result the inside leg grips upwards to try and help keep the rider secure and to prevent any further slipping. It's also often accompanied by the upper body leaning inwards, which actually makes the problem worse.

Outside lower leg swinging forwards This can often happen on circles, especially in canter, when it is often due to centrifugal force causing the seat to slip to the outside. The seat may also slip if the rider draws the inside shoulder or the inside hand back too far, or if the inside rein is too long.

Looking down to one side This fault can be a cause, as well as an indication, of sitting crookedly.

Leaning to one side This allows your seat to slide towards the opposite side. It may be due to an inclination to collapse through one side of your waist as a result of poor posture and one-sidedness, or to the effects of centrifugal force on turns and circles. It can also happen because you are attempting incorrectly to emphasize the effect of the inner seat bone, or to push the leg

on that side down instead of allowing it to stretch down away from the hip. This can also lead to you gripping up with the leg on that side.

One hand higher than the other This can lead to crookedness, as well as being an indication that you are collapsing that side of your waist. This in turn allows your seat to slip in the opposite direction to the side to which you are leaning inwards.

One shoulder higher than the other Again, this is often a sign that you are collapsing through one side of your waist – the lower shoulder will be on that side. The seat will slip towards the side with the higher shoulder.

Off-centre seam The central seam of the jodhpurs is not aligned with the centre of the saddle.

Feeling of slipping to one side Usually the crookedness has become quite extreme by the time you actually feel this unbalanced. You may also find that you are using the rein on the opposite side to which you are slipping to support yourself. There may be a much stronger contact on it than on the other rein, the hand may be clenched into a tight fist, and may even be crossing over the horse's neck in your effort to keep yourself from slipping any further to one side.

One knee or foot higher than the other

When observed by an assistant, this may indicate that you are sitting crookedly – check also that both stirrups are the same length and that the saddle is sitting straight and hasn't slipped to one side. If one foot is pushed further forwards than the other it can look as if the legs are uneven lengths. This is likely to lead to the seat twisting in the saddle and slipping to one side.

Outside shoulder moving too far forwards/inside shoulder moving too far back

Overturning the shoulders or torso to the inside when riding turns, circles or in lateral work is an easily acquired fault, which may also lead to the rider collapsing through the waist and the seat slipping to the outside as a result. Drawing back the outside shoulder instead of remaining square to axis will also lead to crookedness and stiffening through that side of the body, which will be mirrored by the horse. For exercises that will help with Straightness see Chapter 19, Straightness, pp. 190–201.

TIP

If a teacher or friend is available, ask them to check whether your stirrups are the same length while you are mounted. He or she should first check to see that both you and the saddle are straight. Remove both feet from the stirrup irons, since if one foot is pushed further forwards than the other it will give a misleading appearance. The horse should also stand square, or move slowly forwards in a straight line in walk towards the observer.

USEFUL CONTACTS

'The respect of tradition should not prevent the love of progress'

General Alexis L'Holte 1825–1904: French general and riding master

Association of British Riding Schools (ABRS)
38–40 Queens Chambers
Queen Street
Penzance
Cornwall
TR18 4BH
www.abrs-info.org

British Horse Society (BHS)
Stoneleigh Deer Park
Kenilworth
Warwickshire
CV8 2XZ
www.bhs.org.uk

The Pony Club
NAC Stoneleigh Park
Kenilworth
Warwickshire
CV8 2RW
www.pcuk.org

Alexander Technique:
The Society of Teachers of the Alexander
Technique
1st Floor, Linton House
39–51 Highgate Road
London
NW5 1RS
www.stat.org.uk

American Society for the Alexander Technique
PO Box 60008
Florence, MA 01062
www.alexandertech.org

Feldenkrais:
www.feldenkrais.co.uk

Pilates:
Pilates Foundation
Administrator
PO Box 58235
London
N1 5UY
www.pilatesfoundation.com

TTEAM UK
Tilley Farm
Farmborough
Bath
BA2 0AB
www.ttouchtteam.co.uk

TTEAM USA
PO Box 3793
Santa Fe
USA, NM87501
www.lindatellingtonjones.com

British Equestrian Vaulting:
www.vaulting.org.uk

American Equestrian Vaulting Association
AVA National Office
Attention: Craig Coburn
8205 Santa Monica Blvd. #1-288
West Hollywood
CA 90046
www.americanvaulting.org

Connected Riding:
Connected Enterprises, Inc.
PO Box 1627
Poulsbo
Washington 98370
www.connectedriding.com

INDEX

'Riding a horse is a not a gentle hobby, to be picked up and laid down like a game of solitaire. It is a grand passion'

Ralph Waldo Emerson